American Headway 1

Liz and John Soars

OXFORD
UNIVERSITY PRESS

Oxford University Press
198 Madison Avenue
New York, NY 10016 USA

Great Clarendon Street
Oxford OX2 6DP England

Oxford New York

*Athens Auckland Bangkok Bogota Buenos Aires Calcutta
Cape Town Chennai Dar es Salaam Delhi Florence Hong Kong
Istanbul Karachi Kuala Lumpur Madrid Melbourne
Mexico City Mumbai Nairobi Paris São Paulo Shanghai
Singapore Taipei Tokyo Toronto Warsaw*

and associated companies in
Berlin Ibadan

OXFORD is a trademark of Oxford University Press.

Library of Congress Cataloging-in-Publication Data

Soars, Liz
    American headway. Student book 1 / Liz and John Soars.
        p. cm.
    Includes index.
    ISBN 0-19-435375-3
        1. English language—Textbooks for foreign speakers.
2. English language—United States—Problems, exercises, etc.
3. English language—Grammar—Problems, exercises, etc.
4. Vocabulary—Problems, exercises, etc. I. Soars, John,
II. Title.

PE1128 .S5936 2001
428.2'4—dc21   00-051679

No unauthorized photocopying.

American Headway Student Book 1:
Editorial Manager: Shelagh Speers
Managing Editor: Jeff Krum
Editor: Pat O'Neill
Art Director: Lynn Luchetti
Designer: Shelley Himmelstein
Art Buyer/Picture Researcher: Laura Nash
Production Manager: Shanta Persaud
Production Coordinator: Eve Wong

Printing (last digit): 10 9 8 7 6 5 4 3 2 1

Printed in China.

Acknowledgments

Cover concept: Rowie Christopher
Cover design: Rowie Christopher and Silver Editions

Illustrations by Rowie Christopher, Martin Cottam, Roger Fereday,
John Holder, Sarah Jones, Susumu Kawabe, Ian Kellas, Pierre Paul
Pariseau, Andy Parker, Steve Pica, Rodica Prato, Lisa Ringnalda,
Colin Salmon, Stacey Shuett, Anne Stanley, Harry Venning

Handwriting and realia by Kathy Baxendale, Susumu Kawabe

Location and studio photography by Rick Ashley, Gareth Boden,
Haddon Davies, Francisco Rabelo Falcão Jr., Mark Mason, Maggie
Milner, Stephen Ogilvy

*The publishers would like to thank the following for their permission to
reproduce photographs:* Alaska Stock; AMREF; AFP/Corbis; AKG Photos;
Mark Andrew/Getty One Stone; Archive Photos/Image Bank; Art
Resource; Associated Press; Wayne Astep/Getty One Stone; ATC
Productions/Stockmarket; Bruce Ayres/Getty One Stone; David
Baird/Getty One Stone; Barnabys Picture Library; Paul Barton/
Stockmarket; Dave Bartruff/Corbis; Bayer; Bernholtz/Stockmarket;
Bettmann/Corbis; The Hall of Representatives/The Signing of the
Constitution of the United States in 1787, 1940 by Howard Chandler
Christy/Bridgeman Art Library; Pennsylvania Academy of Fine Arts,
Philadelphi/George Washington at Princeton by Charles Willson Peale
1741–1827/Bridgeman Art Library; Jason Childs/FPG; Mike Clement/
Trip Photo Library; D. Cole/Trip Photo Library; Colorific/Telegraph
Colour Library; Dean Conger/Corbis; Corbis; Corbis/Bettmann; Benoit
Decout/Katz; Tony Demi/Robert Harding Picture Library; Di Crollalanza/
Rex Features; George B. Diebold/The Stockmarket; Erik Dreyer/Stone;
Geri Engberg/Stockmarket; European Commission; Greg Balfour
Evans/Greg Evans International; Eyewire; M. Fairman/Trip Photo
Library; Food Features; Foodpix; Gamma Liaison/Corbis; Michael
Goldman/FPG; F. Good/Trip Photo Library; S. Grant/Trip Photo Library;
John Henley/The Stockmarket; Dave Houser/Corbis; David Hughes/
Robert Harding Picture Library; Hulton Getty Picture Collection; Image
Bank; Impact Photos; Insight; Int Stock/Robert Harding Picture Library;
Sian Irving/Anthony Blake Photo Library; Rich Iwasaki/Getty One Stone;
Bob Jacobson/Robert Harding Picture Library; E. James/Trip Photo
Library; Jeff Parry Promotions; John Birdsill Photography; Norma
Joseph/Robert Harding Picture Library; Michael Keller/The Stockmarket;
Sally Lack; Yann Lavma/Getty One Stone; Eric Lessing/AKG Photos;
Rob Lewine/Stockmarket; J. Lightfoot/Robert Harding Picture Library;
Lightscapes Inc./The Stockmarket; Suzanne McCartney; Dennis
McColeman/Getty One Stone; The Mandarin Hotel; Mansell/Katz; Mark
Mawson/Robert Harding Picture Library; N. Menneer/Trip Photo
Library; D. Morgan/Trip Photo Library; Network Photographers; Nick
Oakes/Collections; Ian O'Leary/Getty One Stone; Andrew Olney/Getty
One Stone; K. Owaki/The Stock Market; Jose L. Peleaz/Stockmarket; Pan
American; Panoramic Images; Photodisc; Photo Disk; Pictures; Joseph
Pobereskin/Getty One Stone; Popperfoto; Ulrike Preuss/Format
Photographers; James Randklev/Getty One Stone; David Redfern/
Redferns; Robert Ricci/Gamma Liaison; John Riley/Getty One Stone;
Robert Harding Picture Library; H. Rogers/Trip Photo Library; Martin
Rogers/Getty One Stone; Tom Sanders/Stockmarket; The Savoy Group;
B. Seed/Trip Photo Library; George Shelley/Stockmarket; Simon
Shepherd/Impact Photos; Shotgun/Stockmarket; Juan Silva/Image Bank;
John Sims/Anthony Blake Photo Library; Joseph Sohm/Pan-Am; Susan
Sterner/Associated Press; Mark Stewart/Camera Press; Stockmarket;
Stone; Superstock; Bob Thomas/Getty One Stone; Topham Picturepoint;
Larry Williams/Stockmarket; David Woods/Stockmarket; Jeff Zaruba/The
Stockmarket; Jim Zuckerman/Corbis
Special thanks to Aaron Isquith, Arlette Lurie, Andrea Suffredini, the
Berkeley Carroll School, Brooklyn, NY

*Acknowledgements continue on page 154 which constitutes a continuation
of the copyright page.*

Contents

SCOPE AND SEQUENCE

1 Hello everybody!

am/is/are · my/your/his/her · Everyday objects · Numbers · Hello and good-bye

STARTER ▶

1 Say your names.

> I'm Ali.

> I'm Tomas.

2 Stand up in alphabetical order and say your names.

> I'm Ali.

> I'm Brenda.

> I'm Tomas.

> I'm Zack.

INTRODUCTIONS
am/is/are, my/your

1 **T 1.1** Read and listen.

A Hello. My name's Paula. What's your name?
B Rosa.
A Where are you from, Rosa?
B I'm from Chicago.

T 1.1 Listen and repeat.

GRAMMAR SPOT

name's = name is
what's = what is
I'm = I am

2 Write the conversation.

> **A** Hello. My _____ Gordon. What's _____
> name?
> **B** Jun.
> **A** _____ are you from, Jun?
> **B** _____ from Seoul, South Korea. Where
> _____ you from?
> **A** _____ _____ Toronto, Canada.

T 1.2 Listen and check.

3 Stand up! Talk to the students in the class.

> Hello! My name's _____. What's your name?

> Maria.

> Where are you from, Maria?

> I'm from _____.

Countries, *his/her*

4 **T 1.3** Listen and repeat.

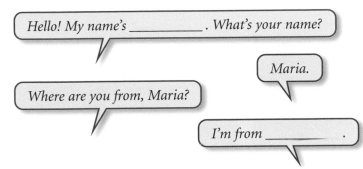

	● ●	● ● ●	● ● ●	● ● ●
the U.S. France	England Russia	Brazil Japan Taiwan	Mexico Canada Italy	Australia Korea

5 Read about the people.

> ¡Hola!

This is Rafael.
He's from Mexico.

> Ninhao!

This is Yaling.
She's from Taiwan.

> Hi!

This is Max and Lisa.
They're from the United States.

GRAMMAR SPOT

he's = he is
she's = she is
they're = they are

6 Where are the people from? Write the countries from Exercise 4.

Hello!

This is Gordon.
_____

Konnichi-wa!

This is Tomoko.
She's from Japan.

Bom dia!

This is Marco and Lena.
_____

Buongiorno!

This is Anna.
_____

Privyet!

This is Irina.
_____

G'day!

This is Jim and Sue.
_____

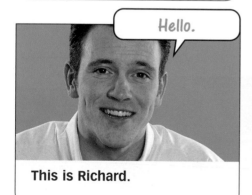

Hello.

This is Richard.
_____

An-nyong ha-se-yo.

This is Jun.
_____

Bonjour!

This is Pierre.
_____

7 Ask and answer questions about the people.
Use *he/his* and *she/her*.

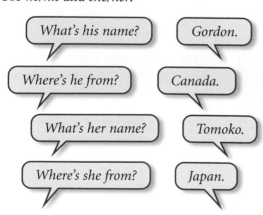

What's his name? Gordon.

Where's he from? Canada.

What's her name? Tomoko.

Where's she from? Japan.

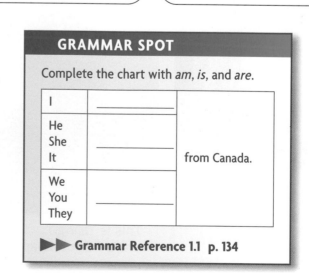

GRAMMAR SPOT

Complete the chart with *am*, *is*, and *are*.

I	_____	
He She It	_____	from Canada.
We You They	_____	

▶▶ **Grammar Reference 1.1 p. 134**

PRACTICE

Talking about you

1 Ask and answer questions with a partner about the students in your class.

> What's his name?

> Where's he from?

2 Introduce your partner to the class.

> This is Jun. She's from Seoul, South Korea.

Listening and pronunciation

3 **T 1.4** Listen and put a check (✓) next to the sentence you hear.

1. ☐ She's from Taiwan.
   ☐ He's from Taiwan.
2. ☐ What's her name?
   ☐ What's his name?
3. ☐ They're from Brazil.
   ☐ They're in Brazil.
4. ☐ Where's she from?
   ☐ Where's he from?
5. ☐ He's a teacher in Italy.
   ☐ His teacher in Italy.

Check it

4 Complete the sentences with *am*, *is*, *are*, *his*, *her*, or *your*.

1. My name __is__ Anna.
2. Where _____ you from?
3. I _____ from Japan.
4. "What's _____ name?" "My name's Tomoko."
5. Max and Lisa _____ from Chicago.
6. This _____ my teacher. _____ name's Gordon.
7. Where _____ he from?
8. This is my sister. _____ name's Anna.

Reading and writing

5 **T 1.5** Read about Rafael and listen.

My name's Rafael Ramos and I'm a doctor. I'm 30. I'm married and I have two children. I live in a house in Toluca in Mexico. I want to learn English for my job.

6 Complete the text about Yaling.

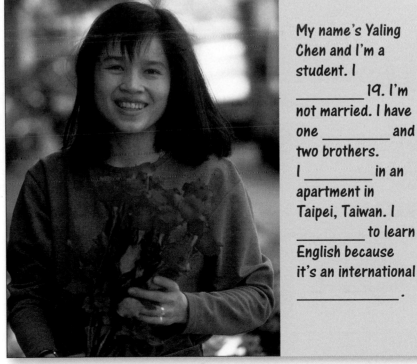

My name's Yaling Chen and I'm a student. I _____ 19. I'm not married. I have one _____ and two brothers. I _____ in an apartment in Taipei, Taiwan. I _____ to learn English because it's an international _____.

T 1.6 Listen and check.

7 Write about *you*. Then read it to the class.

VOCABULARY AND PRONUNCIATION
Everyday objects

1 **T 1.7** Listen to the alphabet song. Say the alphabet as a class.

2 Look at this extract from an English/Spanish dictionary.

the word in English ⟶   the part of speech (n. = noun)

apple /ˈæpl/ n. *manzana*

the pronunciation   the word in Spanish

3 Match the words and pictures.

●●	●●●	●●●●
a stamp a bag a key	a camera a ticket a letter a postcard an apple an orange	a magazine a newspaper	a dictionary

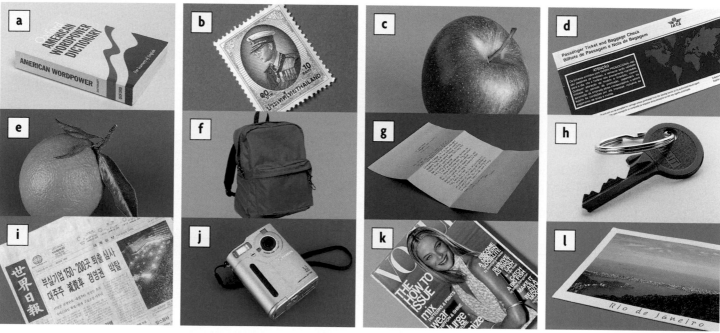

T 1.8 Listen and repeat.

4 Ask and answer questions with a partner.

What's a?

It's a dictionary.

How do you spell that?

D-I-C-T-...

5 Look at the words. What are *a, e, i, o,* and *u*? When do we use *a*? When do we use *an*?

a bag	*an* apple
a ticket	*an* orange
a letter	*an* English book

6 Look at the plural words.

two stamps   two apples   two envelopes

Say the plurals of the other words in Exercise 3.

▶▶ **Grammar Reference 1.4 and 1.5 p. 134**

EVERYDAY ENGLISH
Telephone numbers / Hello and good-bye

1 Say the numbers 1–20 around the class.

2 **T 1.9** Read and listen to the telephone numbers.

726-9304	seven two six nine three oh four
919-677-1303	nine one nine six seven seven one three oh three
1-800-445-9714	one eight hundred four four five nine seven one four

3 **T 1.10** Listen and write the numbers you hear. Practice them.

1. ____**4**____   3. _____   5. _____

2. _____   4. _____   6. _____

4 Ask and answer with other students. Write a list.

> *What's your phone number?*

> *It's (212) 726-6390.*

> *Thank you very much.*

5 Write the conversations in the correct order.

1. Pretty good, thanks.
   Hello. Marty Freeman.
   I'm fine, thanks. And you?
   Hi, Marty. It's Jane. How are you?

   A _Hello. Marty Freeman._
   B _____
   A _____
   B _____

2. Good-bye, Michael.
   Is 7:00 OK with you, Bianca?
   OK. See you then. Good-bye.
   Yes. 7:00 is fine.

   A _____
   B _____
   A _____
   B _____

3. Just fine. How are the children?
   Not bad, thanks. How are you?
   Hello?
   They're fine.
   Hi, Flora! It's me, Leo. How are you?

   A _____
   B _____
   A _____
   B _____
   A _____

T 1.11 Listen and check.

6 Practice the conversations with other students. Practice again, using *your* name and number.

2 Meeting people

am/is/are – questions and negatives · Possessive's · Family · Opposites · In a cafe

STARTER ▶

1 Count from 1–20 around the class.

2 Count in 10s from 10–100 around the class.
ten, twenty, thirty . . . one hundred.

3 How old are you? Ask and answer in groups.

WHO IS SHE?
Questions and negatives

1 Read Keesha Anderson's identity card.

2 Complete the questions.

PERSONAL IDENTITY CARD

LAST NAME *ANDERSON*
FIRST NAME *KEESHA*
COUNTRY *THE UNITED STATES*
JOB *JOURNALIST*
ADDRESS *71 CANYON DRIVE*
LOS ANGELES, CA
PHONE NUMBER *(310) 440-7305*
AGE *28*
MARRIED? *NO*

1. What's **her** last name? Anderson.
2. _____ her first name?   Keesha.
3. _____ she from?   The United States.
4. _____ _____ job?   She's a journalist.
5. What's _____ _____ ?   71 Canyon Drive,
                Los Angeles, California.
6. _____ _____ phone   (310) 440-7305.
   number?
7. How old _____ _____ ? Twenty-eight.
8. Is she _____ ?   No, she isn't.

T 2.1 Listen and check. Practice the questions and answers.

3 **T 2.2** Keesha has a brother. Listen and complete his identity card.

Ask and answer questions with a partner about Keesha's brother.

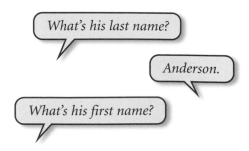

What's his last name?

Anderson.

What's his first name?

PERSONAL IDENTITY CARD

LAST NAME *ANDERSON*
FIRST NAME _____
COUNTRY _____
JOB _____
ADDRESS _____

PHONE NUMBER _____
AGE _____
MARRIED? _____

Negatives and short answers

4 **T 2.3** Read and listen. Then listen and repeat.

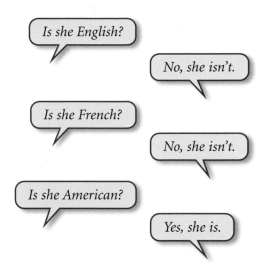

Is she English?

No, she isn't.

Is she French?

No, she isn't.

Is she American?

Yes, she is.

Ask and answer Yes/No questions about Keesha.

1. a doctor? a teacher? a journalist?
2. eighteen? twenty-one? twenty-eight?

5 Ask and answer questions about Keesha's brother.

1. Peter? Daniel? Rick?
2. a journalist? a student? a police officer?
3. sixteen? thirty? twenty-six?

GRAMMAR SPOT

1 Complete the answers to the Yes/No questions.

Is Keesha American?
Yes, she _____ .
Is her last name Smith?
No, it _____ .
Are you a journalist?
No, I'm _____ .

2 Look at the negatives.
She **isn't** married.
You **aren't** English.
But: I**'m not** a teacher
✗ I amn't a teacher.

▶▶ **Grammar Reference 2.1 p. 135**

PRACTICE

Who is he?

1 **Student A** Look at this identity card.
Student B Look at the identity card on page 110.

Ask and answer questions to complete the information.

RBS INTERNATIONAL **IDENTITY CARD**

LAST NAME
FIRST NAME PATRICK
COUNTRY
JOB ACCOUNTANT
ADDRESS

PHONE NUMBER 1232-4837
AGE
MARRIED? YES

2 Ask and answer Yes/No questions about Patrick.
1. Smith? Jones? Binchey?
2. from the United States? from Canada? from Ireland?
3. a police officer? a teacher? an accountant?

Talking about you

3 Ask your teacher some questions.

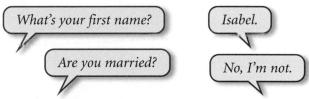

What's your first name?

Isabel.

Are you married?

No, I'm not.

4 Stand up! Ask two students questions to complete the form. Answer questions about you.

	STUDENT 1	STUDENT 2
NAME		
COUNTRY/TOWN		
JOB		
PHONE NUMBER		
AGE		
MARRIED?		

Tell the class about one of the students.

Her name's Carmen. She's a student …

PATRICK'S FAMILY
Possessive 's

1 Write these words in the correct place.

brother	father	daughter	wife	aunt	grandmother

👨	boyfriend	husband			son		uncle	grandfather
👩	*girlfriend*		mother		sister			

2 **T 2.4** Read about Patrick Binchey and listen. Write the names of the people in the correct place.

This is a photo of Patrick, his wife, and his children. His wife's name is Brenda. She's a teacher. His daughter's name is Laura. She's twenty-one and she's a nurse. His son's name is Brian. He's nineteen and he's a student. Laura's boyfriend's name is Mike. He's a nurse, too.

1 _____
2 _____
3 _____
4 _____
5 _____

3 Ask and answer questions about Patrick's family.

Who's Brenda?   *She's Patrick's wife.*

PRACTICE

You and your family

1 Ask your teacher questions about the people in his/her family.

> *What's your mother's name?*

> *What's your sister's name?*

2 Write the names of people in your family. Ask and answer questions with a partner.

Roberto   Silvia   Maria   Fernando   Amelia

Ask a partner questions about his/her family.

> *Who's Roberto?*

> *He's my brother.*

> *Who's Silvia?*

> *She's my aunt.*
> *She's my mother's sister.*

3 Make true sentences with the verb *to be*.

1. I **'m not** at home.
2. We _____ in class.
3. It _____ Monday today.
4. My teacher's name _____ John.
5. My mother and father _____ at work.
6. I _____ married.
7. My grandmother _____ seventy-five years old.
8. Marcos and Carlos _____ my brothers.
9. We _____ in the coffee bar. We _____ in the classroom.

Check it

4 Put a check (✓) next to the correct sentence.

1. ☐ I'm a doctor.
   ☐ I'm doctor.
2. ☐ I have twenty-nine years old.
   ☐ I am twenty-nine years old.
3. ☐ I no married.
   ☐ I'm not married.
4. ☐ My sister's name is Laura.
   ☐ My sisters name is Laura.
5. ☐ She married.
   ☐ She's married.
6. ☐ I'm an uncle.
   ☐ I'm a uncle.
7. ☐ I have two brother.
   ☐ I have two brothers.
8. ☐ Patrick's my sister son's.
   ☐ Patrick's my sister's son.

VOCABULARY
Opposites

1 Match the adjectives with their opposites.

old	awful
big	old
easy	young
new	difficult
fast	cheap
nice	cold
hot	slow
expensive	small

2 Write about the pictures, using the adjectives.

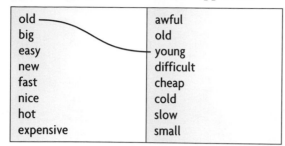

1. He's old.   She's young.

$$2+2=4$$ $$2x^2+2x-8$$

2. _____   _____

3. _____   _____

4. _____   _____

5. _____   _____

6. _____   _____

7. _____   _____

8. _____   _____

T 2.5 Listen and check. Practice saying the sentences.

READING AND LISTENING
A letter from America

1 **T 2.6** Dorita is an English student at a school in New York City. Read and listen to her letter to Miguel, her brother in Argentina.

2 Match each photograph with part of the letter.

3 Correct the false (✗) sentences.
1. Dorita is from Argentina. ✓
2. She's in Miami. ✗ No, she isn't. She's in New York.
3. Dorita's happy in New York.
4. She's on vacation.
5. It's a very big class.
6. The students in her class are all from South America.
7. Annie and Marnie are both students.
8. The subway is easy to use.

4 Write the questions about Dorita's letter.

1. Where's Dorita from _____ ?
   Argentina.
2. _____ ?
   Japan, Brazil, Italy, Taiwan, Mexico, and Russia.
3. _____ ?
   Isabel.
4. _____ ?
   They are sisters. They live with Dorita.
5. _____ ?
   Annie's twenty and Marnie's eighteen.
6. _____ New York _____ ?
   Yes, it is.

5 **T 2.7** Listen to three conversations. Where is Dorita? Who is she with?

Writing

6 Write a letter about *your* class.

1

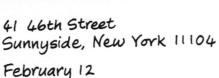

41 46th Street
Sunnyside, New York 11104
February 12

Dear Miguel,

How are you? I'm fine. Here's a letter in English. It's good practice for you and me!

I have classes in English at La Guardia Community College. I'm in a class with eight students. They're all from different countries: Japan, Brazil, Italy, Taiwan, Mexico, and Russia. Our teacher's name is Isabel. She's very nice and a very good teacher.

I live in an apartment with two American girls, Annie and Marnie Kass. They are sisters. Annie's twenty years old and a dancer. Marnie's eighteen and a student. They're very friendly, but it isn't easy to understand them. They speak very fast!

New York is very big and very exciting, but very expensive! The subway isn't hard to use and it's cheap. It's very cold now, but Central Park is beautiful in the snow. I'm very happy here.

Write to me soon.
Love,
Dorita

EVERYDAY ENGLISH

In a cafe

1 1. **T 2.8** Read and listen to the prices.

$1.00 one dollar / a dollar	$10.75 ten dollars and seventy-five cents / ten seventy-five	
$5.00 five dollars	$7.50 seven dollars and fifty cents / seven-fifty	50¢ fifty cents

2. **T 2.9** Write the prices you hear. Practice saying them.

1.   **$5.50**   3. _____   5. _____

2. _____   4. _____   6. _____

2 Read the menu. Match the food and pictures.

SIDNEY'S DELI

♦ ♦ ♦ Menu ♦ ♦ ♦

Hamburger and Fries	$4.75
Grilled Chicken Sandwich	$3.90
Bacon, Lettuce, and Tomato Sandwich	$4.25
Tuna Salad Sandwich	$3.50
Brownie	$1.75
Chocolate Chip Cookie	$1.60
Coffee	$1.00
Tea	$1.00
Orange Juice	$1.50
Bottled Water	$1.25

♦ ♦ ♦ ♦

3 [T 2.10] Listen and repeat. Then ask and answer questions with a partner.

> How much is a hamburger and fries?

> Four dollars and seventy-five cents.

> How much is a hamburger and fries and an orange juice?

> Six twenty-five.

4 [T 2.11] Listen and complete the conversations.

A Good morning.
B Good _____ . Can I have _____ , please?
A Sure. Anything else?
B No thanks.
A A dollar _____ , please.
B Here you go.
A Thank you.

A Hi. Can I help you?
B Yes. Can I have a _____ sandwich, please?
A Anything to drink?
B Yeah. A _____ , please.
A OK. Here you are.
B _____ is that?
A _____ , please.
B OK. Thanks.

5 Practice the conversations with your partner.
Make more conversations.

3 The world of work

Present Simple 1 – *he/she/it* · Questions and negatives · Jobs · What time is it?

STARTER What are the jobs of the people in your family? Tell the class.

> *My father is a doctor.*

> *My mother is a …*

> *My brother …*

THREE JOBS
Present Simple *he/she/it*

1 **T 3.1** Listen and read about David and Pam.

David is a computer scientist. He comes from Taipei in Taiwan, but now he lives in the United States. He works three days a week for Golden Gate Computers in the small town of Lake Forest, California. He speaks three languages: Chinese, English, and Japanese. He's married and has a daughter. He likes playing tennis and riding his bicycle in his free time.

David Lee

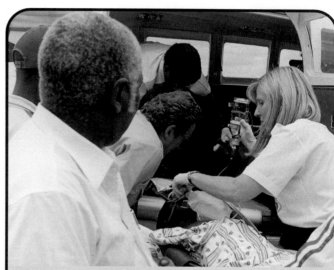

Pam is a doctor. She's Canadian but now she lives in Nairobi, Kenya, in East Africa. She isn't an ordinary doctor—she's a flying doctor. Every day, from 8 A.M. to 10 A.M. she speaks to people on her radio, then she flies to help them. She works 16 hours a day nonstop but she loves her job. She isn't married. She has no free time.

Pam Green

GRAMMAR SPOT

1 Underline all the verbs in the texts.   *is   comes*
2 What is the last letter of these verbs?
3 Practice saying the verbs. Read the texts aloud.

2 Complete the sentences about David and Pam.

1. He's a computer scientist. She __'s__ __a__ doctor.
2. David comes from Taiwan. Pam _____ _____ Canada.
3. She lives in a big city, but he _____ in a _____ town.
4. He _____ three days _____ week. She _____ 16 hours a day _____ .
5. She _____ to sick people on her radio. He _____ three languages.
6. She loves her job and he _____ _____ _____ , too.
7. He _____ _____ daughter. She _____ married.
8. He _____ playing tennis and riding his _____ in his free time. She never _____ free time.

T 3.2 Listen and check.

PRACTICE

Talking about people

1 Read the information about Fernando.

Fernando Costa	
Job	Taxi Driver
Country	Brazil
Town	Fortaleza
Place of work	all over Fortaleza
Languages	Portuguese and a little English
Married?	No
Family	A dog (!)
Free time	walking his dog, playing soccer

2 Talk about Fernando.

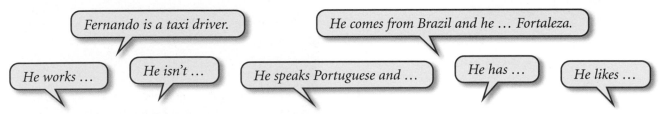

Fernando is a taxi driver.

He comes from Brazil and he ... Fortaleza.

He works ...

He isn't ...

He speaks Portuguese and ...

He has ...

He likes ...

3 Write about a friend or a relative. Talk to a partner about him/her.

My friend Anna is a student. She lives in ...

WHAT DOES SHE DO?
Questions and negatives

1 **T 3.3** Read and listen. Complete the answers. Practice the questions and answers.

Where does David come from?	Taipei, _____ Taiwan.
What does he do?	He's _____ computer scientist.
Does he speak Chinese?	_____ , he does.
Does he speak Spanish?	_____ , he doesn't.

GRAMMAR SPOT

1 What does she/he do? = What's her/his job?

2 Complete these sentences with the correct form of *come*.

Affirmative
He _____ from Taiwan.
Negative
He _____ _____ from Japan.
Question
Where _____ he _____ from?

3 Notice the pronunciation of *does* and *doesn't*.

/dəz/   /dʌz/   /'dʌznt/
Does he speak Chinese? Yes he **does**./No, he **doesn't**.

▶▶ **Grammar Reference 3.1 p. 136**

---

2 Complete the questions and answers.

1. Where _____ Pam _____ from?
   Canada.
2. What _____ she _____ ?
   She's a doctor.
3. _____ she fly to help people?
   Yes, she _____ .
4. _____ she _____ Chinese and Japanese?
   No, she _____ .

T 3.4 Listen and check.

3 Write similar questions about Fernando the taxi driver. Ask and answer with a partner.

> *Where does Fernando come from?*

> *Fortaleza.*

PRACTICE
Asking about people

1 Read the information about Keiko or Mark.

Keiko Wilson

Job	an interpreter
Country	Japan
Town	New York
Place of work	at the United Nations
Languages	Japanese, English, and French
Family	married to an American, two sons
Free time	skiing

2 Talk to a partner.

> *Keiko's an interpreter. She comes from Japan. She lives …*

3 Write questions about Keiko or Mark.

- Where/come from?
  Where does Keiko come from?
- Where/live?
- What/do?
- Where/work?
- Does he/she speak French/Spanish . . .?
- What . . . in his/her free time?
- . . . listen to music?
- How many children . . .?
- . . . a dog?

4 *Don't* look at the information. Ask and answer questions with your partner.

5 Now ask your partner the same questions about a friend or relative.

Listening and pronunciation

6 **T 3.5** Listen to the sentences about Fernando, Keiko, and Mark. Correct the wrong sentences.

Fernando comes from Brazil.

Yes, that's right.

Fernando lives in New York.

No, he doesn't. He lives in Fortaleza.

7 **T 3.6** Put a check (✓) next to the sentence you hear.

1. ☐ He likes his job.
   ☐ She likes her job.
2. ☐ She loves walking.
   ☐ She loves working.
3. ☐ He's married.
   ☐ He isn't married.
4. ☐ Does she have three children?
   ☐ Does he have three children?
5. ☐ What does he do?
   ☐ Where does he go?

Check it

8 Put a check (✓) next to the correct sentence.

1. ☐ She comes from Japan.
   ☐ She come from Japan.
2. ☐ What he do in his free time?
   ☐ What does he do in his free time?
3. ☐ Where lives she?
   ☐ Where does she live?
4. ☐ He isn't married.
   ☐ He doesn't married.
5. ☐ Does she has two sons?
   ☐ Does she have two sons?
6. ☐ He doesn't play soccer.
   ☐ He no plays soccer.
7. ☐ She doesn't love Peter.
   ☐ She doesn't loves Peter.
8. ☐ What's he's address?
   ☐ What's his address?

Mark Kingman

Job	a journalist for CNN
Country	U.S.
Town	Moscow
Place of work	in an office
Languages	English, Russian, and German
Family	married, three daughters
Free time	playing tennis

READING AND LISTENING

Seamus McSporran—the man with thirteen jobs!

1 **Seamus McSporran** /ˈʃeɪməs məkˈspɑrən/ comes from Scotland. Look at the photographs of some of the things he does every day.

6:00 A.M.

8:00 A.M.

The man with thirteen jobs

9:00 A.M.

10:00 A.M.

12:00 A.M.

2:00 P.M.

3:00 P.M.

5:00 P.M.

2 Match a sentence to a photograph.

   _h_ 1. He **helps** in the shop.

   ____ 2. He **makes** breakfast for the hotel guests.

   ____ 3. He **pumps** gas.

   ____ 4. He **delivers** beer to the pub.

   ____ 5. He **gets** the mail from the boat.

   ____ 6. He **drives** the children to school.

   ____ 7. He **delivers** the mail.

   ____ 8. He **has** a glass of wine.

   ____ 9. He **works** as an undertaker.

SEAMUS McSPORRAN is a very busy man. He is 60 years old and he has 13 jobs. He is a mail carrier, a police officer, a fire fighter, a taxi driver, a schoolbus driver, a boatman, an ambulance driver, an accountant, a gas station attendant, a bartender, and an undertaker. Also, he and his wife, Margaret, have a shop and a small hotel.

Seamus lives and works on the island of Gigha /ˈgiyə/ in the west of Scotland. Only 120 people live on the island but in the summer 150 tourists come by boat every day.

Every weekday Seamus gets up at 6:00 and makes breakfast for the hotel guests. At 8:00 he drives the island's children to school. At 9:00 he gets the mail from the boat and delivers it to all the houses on the island. He also delivers beer to the island's only pub. Then he helps Margaret in the shop.

He says: "Margaret likes being busy, too. We never take vacations and we don't like watching television. In the evenings Margaret makes supper and I pay the bills. At 10:00 we have a glass of wine and then we go to bed. Perhaps our life isn't very exciting, but we like it."

10:00 P.M.

3 Read about Seamus. Answer the questions.
1. Where does Seamus live?
2. How old is he?
3. How many jobs does he have?
4. What's his wife's name?
5. What does she do?
6. How many people live on the island of Gigha?
7. How many tourists visit Gigha in the summer?
8. What does Seamus do in the morning?
9. What do he and Margaret do in the evening?

4 Look at the photographs. Ask and answer questions with a partner about times in Seamus's day.

> *What does he do at 6 o'clock?*

> *He gets up and makes breakfast.*

5 **T 3.7** Listen to four conversations from Seamus's day. After each one answer these questions.
1. Is it morning, afternoon, or evening?
2. Who are the people? Where are they?
3. What is Seamus's job?

6 Complete the conversations.
1. **A** Good _____ . Can I _____ two ice creams, please?
   B Chocolate or vanilla?
   A One chocolate, one vanilla, please.
   B That's £1.80. Anything _____ ?
   A No, thank you.

2. **A** Only _____ letters for you this _____ , Mrs. Craig.
   B Thank you very much, Mr. McSporran. And _____'s Mrs. McSporran this _____ ?
   A Oh, she's very well, thank you. She's _____ in the shop.

3. **A** A glass of _____ before bed, my dear?
   B Oh, yes please.
   A _____ you are.
   B Thank you, my dear. I'm very _____ this _____ .

4. **A** Hello, Mr. McSporran!
   B Good _____ , boys and girls. Hurry up, we're late.
   A Can I sit here, Mr. McSporran?
   C No, no, I _____ to sit there.
   B Be quiet _____ of you, and SIT DOWN!

Practice the conversations with your partner.

VOCABULARY AND PRONUNCIATION
Jobs

1 Use your dictionary and match a picture with a job in Column **A**.

1 | d |

2 | |

3 | | 4 | | 5 | |

6 | | 7 | | 8 | |

9 | |

	A	B
a.	A pilot	designs buildings.
b.	An interpreter	cooks food.
c.	A nurse	takes care of people in the hospital.
d.	A bartender	takes care of people's money.
e.	An accountant	writes for a newspaper.
f.	A journalist	translates things.
g.	A chef	sells things.
h.	An architect	flies planes.
i.	A sales assistant	serves drinks.

2 Match a job in **A** with a line in **B**.

3 Memorize the jobs. Close your books. Ask and answer questions with a partner.

> *What does a pilot do?*

> *He/She flies planes.*

EVERYDAY ENGLISH

What time is it?

1 Look at the clocks. Write the times. Practice saying them.

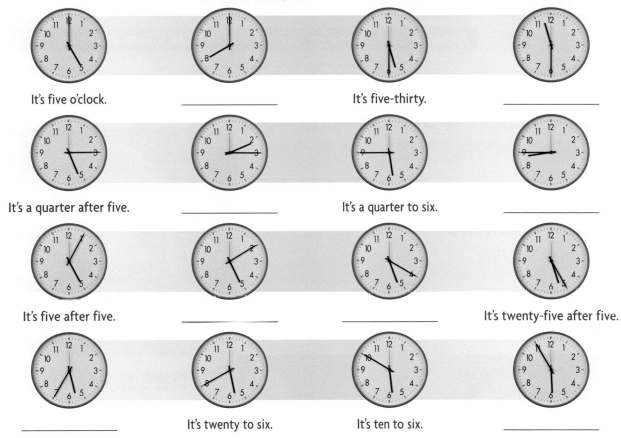

It's five o'clock.

_____

It's five-thirty.

_____

It's a quarter after five.

_____

It's a quarter to six.

_____

It's five after five.

_____

_____

It's twenty-five after five.

_____

It's twenty to six.

It's ten to six.

_____

T 3.8 Listen and check.

2 Look at the times.

It's about three o'clock.   It's about five o'clock.

What time is it now? What time does the class end?

3 **T 3.9** Listen and practice the conversations.

Conversation 1

Excuse me. Do you know what time it is?

Yes. It's about six o'clock.

Thanks.

Conversation 2

Excuse me. Do you know what time it is?

I'm sorry, I don't know. I don't have a watch.

That's OK. Thanks anyway.

With a partner, draw clocks on a piece of paper. Make more conversations.

4 Take it easy!

Present Simple 2 – I/you/we/they · Leisure activities · Social expressions

STARTER ▶

1 What year is it? What month is it? What day is it today?

2 Say the days of the week. Which days are the weekend?

WEEKDAYS AND WEEKENDS
Present Simple *I/you/we/they*

1 Read about Bobbi Brown's weekends. Complete the text with the verbs.

| gets up   lives   is   loves   works   doesn't work   interviews   starts |

"What's free time?"

says Bobbi Brown.

Bobbi's weekends

Bobbi Brown ___lives___ in New Jersey. She _____ thirty-four and _____ for the Manhattan News Network in New York City. But she _____ on weekdays, she only works on weekends. She _____ famous people for an early morning news program called *The World This Weekend.* On Saturday and Sunday she _____ at 3:00 in the morning because she _____ work at 6:30! She _____ her job because it is exciting.

2 [T 4.1] Now read and listen to what Bobbi says about her weekdays.

" *My weekends are busy and exciting. My weekdays at home are busy, too! I __have__ two sons, Dylan, 7, and Dakota, 5. Every morning I _____ one hour before them, at 6:00, and I _____ to the gym. I _____ home and I _____ breakfast. Then I _____ them to school. On Mondays I always _____ . I _____ all the food for the week. I often _____ dinner in the evenings, but not every day because I don't _____ cooking. Fortunately, my husband, Don, _____ cooking. On Tuesdays and Thursdays I _____ my father. He _____ on the next block. Every afternoon I _____ the kids from school. In the evenings Don and I usually _____ , but sometimes we _____ friends. We never _____ on Friday evenings because I _____ work so early on Saturdays.* "

3 Complete the text with the correct form of the verbs in the box. Look up new words in your dictionary.

love	relax	have	like	go	live
start	come	visit (x2)	go shopping	pick up	go out
get up	take	buy	make	cook	

[T 4.1] Listen again and check. Read the text aloud.

Questions and negatives

4 [T 4.2] Read and listen. Complete Bobbi's answers. Practice the questions and answers.

Where do you work? _____ New York.
Do you like your work? Yes, I _____ .
Do you relax on weekends? No, I _____ .
Why don't you relax on weekends? _____ I work.

5 Work in pairs. One of you is Bobbi Brown. Ask and answer questions about your life.

- Where . . . you live/work?
- Are . . . married?
- Do . . . have children?
- What time . . . get up/Saturday morning/Monday morning?
- Why . . . get up at . . . ? Because I . . .
- . . . like your work?
- Why . . . like it? Because it . . .
- . . . like cooking?
- . . . your husband like cooking?
- Who . . . you visit on Tuesdays and Thursdays?
- Where . . . your father live?
- . . . go out on Friday evenings? Why not?
- . . . have a busy life?

GRAMMAR SPOT

1 Complete the chart for the Present Simple.

	Affirmative	Negative
I	work	don't work
You	_____	_____
He/She	_____	_____
It	_____	_____
We	_____	_____
They	_____	_____

2 Complete the questions and answers.

Where _____ you work?
Where _____ she work?
_____ you work in New York? Yes, I _____ .
_____ he work in New York? No, he _____ .

3 Find these words in the text:
always usually often sometimes never

▶▶ **Grammar Reference 4.1 and 4.2 p. 137**

PRACTICE

Talking about you

1 Make the questions. Then match the questions and answers.

Questions		Answers
1. What time	do you like your job?	a. My mother and sisters.
2. Where	do you travel to school?	b. To Hawaii or California.
3. What	do you go on vacation?	c. After dinner.
4. When	do you go to bed?	d. At 11:00.
5. Who	you go out on Friday evenings?	e. I always relax.
6. Why	do you live with?	f. Because it's interesting.
7. How	do you do on Sundays?	g. By bus.
8. Do	do you do your homework?	h. Yes, I do sometimes.

T 4.3 Listen and check.

2 Ask and answer the questions with a partner. Give true answers.

3 Tell the class about you and your partner.

Maria gets up at 8:30. I get up at 8:00 on weekdays but at 11:00 on the weekend.

I live with my parents and my grandmother. Maria lives with her parents, too.

Listening and pronunciation

4 **T 4.4** Put a check (✓) next to the sentence you hear.

1. ☐ What does he do on Sundays?
   ☐ What does she do on Sundays?

2. ☐ Do you stay home on Tuesday evenings?
   ☐ Do you stay home on Thursday evenings?

3. ☐ He lives here.
   ☐ He leaves here.

4. ☐ Where do you go on Saturday evenings?
   ☐ What do you do on Saturday evenings?

5. ☐ I read a lot.
   ☐ I eat a lot.

6. ☐ Why do you like your job?
   ☐ Why don't you like your job?

A questionnaire

5 Read the questionnaire on page 27. Answer the questions about you. Put a ✓ or an ✗ in Column 1.

6 Ask your teacher the questions, then ask two students. Complete columns 2, 3, and 4.

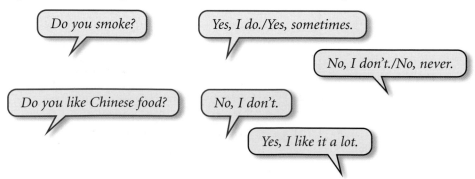

Do you smoke?

Yes, I do./Yes, sometimes.

No, I don't./No, never.

Do you like Chinese food?

No, I don't.

Yes, I like it a lot.

7 Use the information in the questionnaire. Write about you and your teacher.
I don't get up early on weekdays, but my teacher does. We don't play tennis ...

A Questionnaire

HOW DO YOU LIVE?

Do you ... ?	You	Your Teacher	Student 1	Student 2
get up early on weekdays	☐	☐	☐	☐
play tennis	☐	☐	☐	☐
smoke	☐	☐	☐	☐
drink wine	☐	☐	☐	☐
like Chinese food	☐	☐	☐	☐
watch TV a lot	☐	☐	☐	☐
have a big breakfast	☐	☐	☐	☐
have a computer	☐	☐	☐	☐

Affirmatives and negatives

8 Make the sentences opposite.

1. She's French. *She isn't French.*
2. I don't like cooking. *I like cooking.*
3. She doesn't speak Spanish.
4. They want to learn English.
5. We're tired and want to go to bed.
6. Roberto likes watching soccer on TV, but he doesn't like playing it.
7. I work at home because I have a computer.
8. Amelia isn't happy because she doesn't have a new car.
9. They smoke, they drink, and they don't go to bed early.
10. He doesn't smoke, he doesn't drink, and he goes to bed early.

READING AND LISTENING
My favorite season

1 1. What season is it now? What are the seasons?
2. What month is it now? Say the months of the year.
3. When are the different seasons in your country?

2 Look at the photographs. Which season is it? What colors do you see?

3 **T 4.5** Read and listen to three people from different countries.

AL WHEELER
from Canada

We have long, cold winters and short, hot summers. I have a vacation home, or cottage, as we say here. It's near a lake, so in the summer I go sailing a lot and I play baseball. In the winter I often play ice hockey and go ice-skating. My favorite season is fall. I love the colors of the trees—red, gold, orange, yellow, and brown.

MARISOL GONZALEZ
from Florida

People think it's always warm and sunny in Florida, but January and February are often wet and gray. I don't like winter. I usually meet friends in restaurants and clubs. Sometimes we go to a Cuban club. I love Cuban music. But then suddenly it's summer again and on weekends we go to the beach, sunbathe, and go swimming. I love summer.

TOSHI SUZUKI from Japan

I work for Pentax cameras, in the export department. I don't have a lot of free time, but I have one special hobby—taking photographs, of course! I like taking photographs of flowers, especially in the spring. Sometimes, after work, I relax in a club near my office with friends. My friend Shigeru likes singing Karaoke. I don't sing—I'm too shy!

4 Answer the questions.

1. Do they all play sports?
2. What do Al and Marisol do in winter?
3. Do Marisol and Toshi like going to clubs?
4. Where is Al's vacation home?
5. When does Toshi like taking photographs of flowers?
6. What do Marisol and her friends do in the summer?
7. Do you know all their jobs?
8. Why does Al like the fall?
9. Why doesn't Toshi sing in the bar?
10. Which colors are mentioned in the texts?

5 There are six mistakes about Al, Marisol, and Toshi. Correct them.

Al comes from Canada. In winter he plays ice hockey and goes skiing. He has a vacation home near the ocean.	**Marisol** comes from Cuba. She likes sunbathing and sailing in summer.	**Toshi** comes from Japan. He has a lot of free time. He likes taking photographs and singing songs in clubs.

6 **T 4.6** Listen to the conversations. Is it Al, Marisol, or Toshi? Where are they? How do you know? Discuss with a partner.

What do you think?

- What is *your* favorite season? Why?
- What do *you* do in the different seasons?

VOCABULARY AND SPEAKING
Leisure activities

1 Match the words and pictures. Put a check (✓) next to the things that *you* like doing.

☐ going to the gym
☐ dancing
☐ skiing
☐ watching TV
☐ playing soccer
☐ taking photographs
☐ cooking
☐ playing computer games
☐ sailing
☐ listening to music
☐ swimming
☐ reading
☐ eating in restaurants
☐ going to the movies
☐ jogging
☐ sunbathing

2 Discuss in groups what you think your teacher likes doing. Choose *five* activities.

> *I think he/she likes cooking.*

> *No, I think he/she likes eating in restaurants.*

Ask your teacher questions to find out who is correct.

> *Do you like cooking?*

> *Do you like eating in restaurants?*

3 Tell the other students what you *like* doing and what you *don't like* doing from the list. Ask questions about the activities.

> *I don't like watching TV, but I like reading very much.*

> *Oh, really? What do you read?*

> *Why don't you like watching TV?*

4 Tell the other students things you like doing that are *not* on the list.

EVERYDAY ENGLISH

Social expressions

1 Complete the conversations with the expressions.

---

1. **A** _____ . The traffic is bad today.

    B _____ . Come and sit down. We're on page 35.

    That's OK.

    I'm sorry I'm late.

---

2. **A** _____ .

    B Yes?

    A Do you have a pencil?

    B _____ . I only have a pen.

    A Oh, OK. _____ .

    I'm sorry.

    Excuse me.

    Thanks anyway.

---

3. **A** It's very hot in here. _____ ?

    B _____ ? I'm kind of cold.

    A OK. _____ .

    Really?

    Can I open the window?

    It doesn't matter.

---

4. **A** _____ .

    B Can I help you?

    A Can I have some film for my camera?

    B How many exposures?

    A _____ ?

    B How many exposures?

    A _____ ?

    B How many pictures? 24? 36?

    A Ah! _____ !
    Twenty-four, please.

    Pardon?

    Now I understand!

    Excuse me.

    What does *exposures* mean?

T 4.7 Listen and check.

2 Practice the conversations with a partner.

5 Where do you live?

There is/are · Prepositions · some/any · this/that · Furniture · Directions 1

STARTER

1 Write the words in the correct column.

an armchair   a refrigerator   a television
a coffee table   a shelf   a plant   a stereo
a lamp   an oven   a dishwasher   a closet
a telephone   a cabinet   a cup   a sofa

The living room	The kitchen	Both
an armchair		

2 What's in your living room?
Tell a partner.

WHAT'S IN THE LIVING ROOM?
There is/are, prepositions

1 Describe the living room on page 33.

> *There's a telephone.*

> *There are three plants.*

2 **T 5.1** Read and listen. Complete the answers.
Practice the questions and answers.

Is there a television?	Yes, there _____ .
Is there a radio?	No, there _____ .
Are there any books?	Yes, there _____ .
How many books are there?	There _____ a lot.
Are there any photographs?	No, there _____ .

GRAMMAR SPOT

Complete the charts.

Affirmative

There	_____	a television.
	_____	some books.

Negative

There	_____	a radio.
	_____	any photographs.

Question

_____	there	a radio?
_____		any books?

▶▶ **Grammar Reference 5.1 and 5.2 p. 137**

3 Ask and answer questions about these things.

a dog	a cat	a computer
a balcony	a mirror	a lamp
a rug		

plants	pictures	bookshelves
clocks	newspapers	photos
flowers		

> *Is there a dog?*

> *Yes, there is.*

4 Look at the picture of Helen's living room.
Complete the sentences with a preposition.

on	under	next to	in front of

1. The television is __on__ the table.
2. The coffee table is _____ the sofa.
3. There are some magazines _____ the table.
4. The television is _____ the stereo.
5. There are some pictures _____ the walls.
6. The dog is _____ the rug _____ the armchair.

Helen's living room

PRACTICE

Complete your picture

1 **Student A** Look at the picture of the living room on page 111. *Don't* look at your partner's picture.

Student B Look at the picture of the living room on page 112. *Don't* look at your partner's picture.

2 **T 5.2** Look at your complete picture. Listen to someone describing it. There are *five* mistakes in the description. Say "Stop!" when you hear a mistake.

> *Stop! There aren't three people! There are four people!*

WHAT'S IN THE KITCHEN?

some/any, this/that/these/those

1 This is the kitchen in Helen's new apartment. Describe it.

Helen's kitchen

2 **T 5.3** Listen and complete the conversation between Helen and her friend Bob.

Helen And this is the kitchen.

Bob Wow ... it's really nice.

Helen Well, it's not very big, but there _____ a _____ of cabinets. And _____'s a new refrigerator, and an oven. That's new, too.

Bob But what's *in* all these cabinets?

Helen Well, not a lot. There are some cups, but there aren't any plates. And I have _____ knives and forks, but I don't have _____ spoons!

Bob Do you have _____ glasses?

Helen No, I don't.

Bob That's OK. We can drink this champagne from those cups! Cheers!!

3 What is there in *your* kitchen? How is your kitchen different from Helen's?

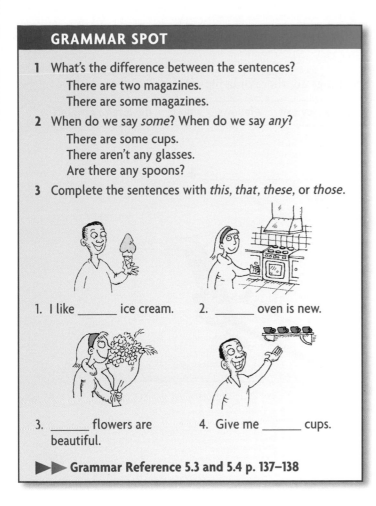
PRACTICE

In our classroom

1 Complete the sentences with *some* or *any*.

1. In our classroom there are ___**some**___ books on the floor.
2. There aren't _____ plants.
3. Are there _____ Chinese students in your class?
4. There aren't _____ Spanish students.
5. We have _____ pencils in the cabinet.
6. There aren't _____ pens in my bag.

2 What is there in your classroom? Describe it.

3 Talk about things in your classroom, using *this/that/these/those*. Point to or hold the things.

This is my favorite pen.

I like that bag.

These chairs are nice.

Those windows are dirty.

What's in Yoshi's briefcase?

4 **T 5.4** Yoshi is on business in Los Angeles. Listen to him describe what's in his briefcase. Put a check (✓) next to the things in it.

- ✓ a newspaper
- ☐ a sandwich
- ☐ a dictionary
- ☐ pens
- ☐ a bus ticket
- ☐ a notebook
- ☐ stamps
- ☐ keys
- ☐ an envelope
- ☐ photos
- ☐ an address book
- ☐ a cell phone

5 Look in *your* bag. Ask and answer questions about your bags with a partner.

Is there a dictionary in your bag?

Are there any stamps?

How many stamps are there?

Check it

6 Put a check (✓) next to the correct sentence.

1. ☐ There aren't some sandwiches.
   ☐ There aren't any sandwiches.
2. ☐ Do you have some good dictionary?
   ☐ Do you have a good dictionary?
3. ☐ I have some photos of my dog.
   ☐ I have any photos of my dog.
4. ☐ I have lot of books.
   ☐ I have a lot of books.
5. ☐ How many students are there in this class?
   ☐ How many of students are there in this class?
6. ☐ Next my house there's a park.
   ☐ Next to my house there's a park.
7. ☐ Look at this house over there!
   ☐ Look at that house over there!
8. ☐ Henry, that is my mother. Mom, that is Henry.
   ☐ Henry, this is my mother. Mom, this is Henry.

READING AND SPEAKING
At home on a plane

1 Write the words in the correct place on the picture. What other things are there on a plane?

| steps | the cockpit | a flight attendant | the first class section | an emergency exit | windows | a door | the lavatory (toilet) |

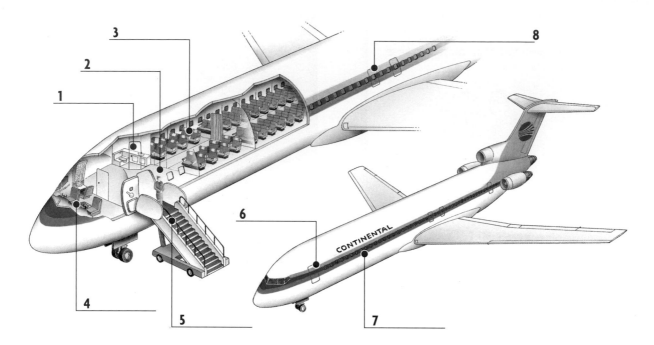

2 Read about Joanne Ussery and answer the questions.

1. How old is she?
2. Where does she live?
3. How old is her home?
4. How many grandsons does she have?
5. How many bedrooms are there?
6. How many toilets are there?

3 Are the sentences true (✔) or false (✘)?

1. Joanne loves her home.
2. You need a ticket when you visit her.
3. The bathroom is next to the living room.
4. Joanne sometimes opens the emergency exit doors.
5. There is a photo of the plane in the living room.
6. It's very warm in the summer because she doesn't have air conditioning.
7. Her friends love her parties because flight attendants serve the drinks.
8. She doesn't want to buy another plane.

4 Work with a partner. Ask and answer questions about Joanne's home.

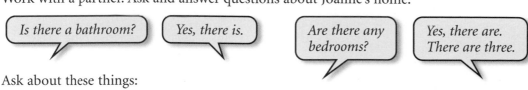

Is there a bathroom?   *Yes, there is.*   *Are there any bedrooms?*   *Yes, there are. There are three.*

Ask about these things:

- a telephone
- a dishwasher
- toilets
- flight attendants
- an upstairs bedroom

What do you think?

What do you like about Joanne's home? What don't you like?

The lady who lives on a plane

Joanne Ussery, 54, from Benoit, Mississippi, is a big favorite with her two grandsons because she lives on a jet plane. Her home is a Boeing 727, so a visit to Grandma is very special.

Joanne's front door is at the top of the plane's steps, but you don't need a ticket or a passport when you visit. There are three bedrooms, a living room, a modern kitchen, and a luxury bathroom. The bathroom is in the cockpit, with the bathtub under the windows. Next to this is Joanne's bedroom—in the first class section of the plane. Then there's the living room with four emergency exit doors, which she opens on summer evenings. On the wall there's a photo of the plane flying for Continental Airlines from Florida to the Caribbean. There are also four toilets, all with No Smoking signs.

"The plane is 27 years old and it's the best home in the world," says Joanne. "It has all the things you want in a home: a telephone, air conditioning, an oven, a washing machine, even a dishwasher. It's always very warm, even in winter, and it's very big, 42 meters long! My grandchildren love running up and down. And my friends love parties here—but there aren't any flight attendants to serve them their drinks!"

The plane cost Joanne just $2,000. "Next time," she says, "I want a Boeing 747, not a 727, because they have an upstairs and a downstairs, and I want to go upstairs to bed!" ✈

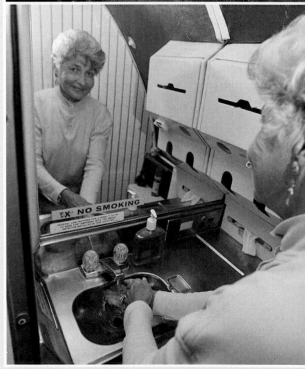

LISTENING AND SPEAKING
Homes around the world

1 Match the photos and places. What do you know about these places?

___ Lisbon, Portugal ___ Toronto, Ontario ___ Malibu, California ___ Samoa

2 **T 5.5** Listen to some people from these places. Complete the chart.

c

a

b

d

	Manola from LISBON	**Ray and Elsie** from TORONTO	**Brad** from MALIBU	**Alise** from SAMOA
House or apartment?	apartment			
Old or modern?				
Where?				
How many bedrooms?				
Live(s) with?				
Extra information				

3 Talk about where *you* live.

> *Do you live in a house or an apartment?*

> *Where is it?*

> *How many rooms are there?*

> *Do you have a yard?*

> *Who do you live with?*

4 Write a paragraph about where you live.

EVERYDAY ENGLISH
Directions 1

1 Look at the street map. Where can you buy these things?

| some aspirin   a CD   a plane ticket   a newspaper   a book   some stamps |

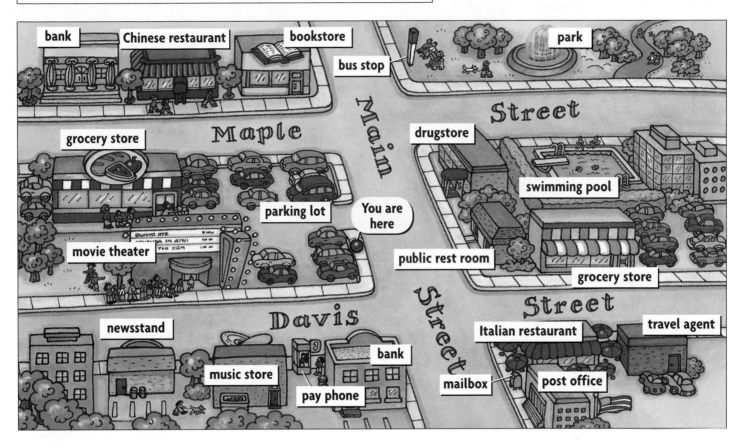

2 **T 5.6** Listen to the conversations and complete them.

1. **A** Excuse me. Is <u>there</u> a drugstore _____ here?
   B Yes. It's over _____ .
   A Thanks.

2. **A** _____ me. Is there a _____ near here?
   B Yes, _____ _____ Davis Street. Just go straight and then _____ _____ on Davis. It's _____ _____ the music store.
   A OK. Thanks.

3. **A** Excuse me. Is there a _____ near here?
   B There's a Chinese one on Maple Street, _____ _____ the bank, and there's an Italian one on Davis Street next to the _____ _____ .
   A Is that one _____ ?
   B No. It's just a block away. It takes two minutes, that's all.

4. **A** Is there a post office near here?
   B Go straight ahead. It's _____ _____ left, next to the Italian restaurant.
   A Thanks a lot.

Practice the conversations with a partner.

3 Make more conversations with your partner. Ask and answer about these places:

- a bookstore
- a movie theater
- a bank
- a pay phone
- a public rest room
- a music store
- a grocery store
- a bus stop
- a park
- a swimming pool
- a mailbox

4 Talk about where *you* are. Is there a drugstore near here? Is it far? What about a bank/a post office/ a grocery store?

6 Can you speak English?

STARTER

1 Where do people speak these languages?

Spanish   French   Chinese   Portuguese   Japanese   English

> *They speak Spanish in Spain and also in Mexico.*

2 Which languages can you speak?
Tell the class.

> *I can speak English and a little Spanish. And of course, I can speak my language.*

WHAT CAN YOU DO?
can/can't

1 **T 6.1** Match the sentences with the pictures. Then listen and check.

1. He can ski really well.
2. She can use a computer.
3. "Can dogs swim?" "Yes, they can."
4. "Can you speak Japanese?" "No, I can't."
5. I can't spell your name.
6. We can't understand the question.

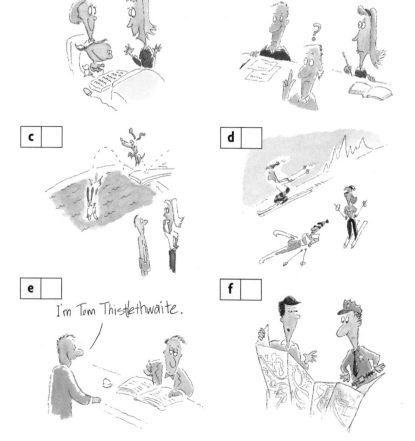

a			b	
c			d	
e			f	

I'm Tom Thistlethwaite.

GRAMMAR SPOT

1 Say all persons of *can* and *can't*.

I can, you can, he ... she ... it ... we ... they ...
I can't, you ... , etc.

What do you notice?

2 **T 6.2** Listen and repeat these sentences.

I can speak Spanish.
Can you speak Spanish?   = /kən/
Yes, I can.   = /kæn/
No, I can't.   = /kænt/

3 Say these sentences.

● ● ●   ● ● ●

We can swim.   She can't cook.

▶▶ **Grammar Reference 6.1 p. 138**

2 **T 6.3** Listen and complete the sentences with *can* or *can't* + verb.

1. I _can_ _speak_ _____ , but I _____ _____ _____ .
2. He _____ _____ , but he _____ _____ .
3. "_____ you _____ ?" "Yes, I _____ ."
4. They _____ _____ , but they _____ _____ .
5. We _____ _____ and we _____ _____ .
6. "_____ she _____ ?" "No, she _____ ."

PRACTICE

Tina can't cook. Can you?

1 **T 6.4** Listen to Tina and complete the chart. Put a ✓ or an ✗.

Can ...?	Tina	you	your partner
drive a car	✗		
speak French			
speak Spanish			
cook			
play tennis			
swim			
ski			
play the piano			
use a computer			

2 Complete the chart about you.

3 Complete the chart about your partner. Ask and answer the questions.

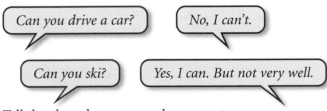

Can you drive a car?   *No, I can't.*

Can you ski?   *Yes, I can. But not very well.*

Tell the class about you and your partner.

Luis can ski, but I can't.

What can computers do?

4 Talk about computers with a partner. What can they do? What can't they do?

They can translate, but they can't speak English.

Yes, they can.

COMPUTERS

Can they . . . ?

- translate
- write poetry
- speak English
- laugh
- play chess
- hear
- check spellings
- feel
- make music
- think
- have conversations
- fall in love

5 What can people do that computers can't do?

WHERE WERE YOU YESTERDAY?

was/were, can/could

Read the questions. Complete the answers.

Present	Past
1. What day is it today? It's _____ .	What day was it yesterday? It was _____ .
2. What month is it now? It's _____ .	What month was it last month? It was _____ .
3. Where are you now? I'm in/at _____ .	Where were you yesterday? I was in/at _____ .
4. Are you in the United States? _____ , I am. _____ , I'm not.	Were you in the U.S. in 2000? _____ , I was. _____ , I wasn't.
5. Can you swim? _____ , I can. _____ , I can't.	Could you swim when you were five? _____ , I could. _____ , I couldn't.
6. Can your teacher speak three languages? Yes, _____ can. No, _____ can't.	Could your teacher speak English when he/she was seven? Yes, _____ could. No, _____ couldn't.

GRAMMAR SPOT

1 Complete the table with the past of *to be*.

	Affirmative	Negative
I	was	wasn't
You	were	weren't
He/She/It	_____	_____
We	_____	_____
They	_____	_____

2 **T 6.5** Listen and repeat.

/wəz/   /wər/
It was Monday yesterday. We were at school.

/wəz/   /wʌz/
"Was it hot?"   *"Yes, it was."*

/wər/   /wər/
"Were you tired?"   *"Yes, we were."*

3 What is the past of *can*?

Affirmative _____   **Negative** _____

▶▶ **Grammar Reference 6.1 and 6.2 p. 138**

PRACTICE

Talking about you

1 Ask and answer questions with a partner.
Where were you . . . ?

- at eight o'clock this morning
- at six-thirty yesterday evening
- at two o'clock this morning
- at this time yesterday
- at ten o'clock last night
- last Saturday evening

2 Complete the conversation using *was, were, wasn't, weren't,* or *couldn't.*

Kim	**Were** you at Carol's party last Saturday?
Max	Yes, I _____ .
Kim	_____ it good?
Max	Well, it _____ OK.
Kim	_____ there many people?
Max	Yes, there _____ .
Kim	_____ Henry there?
Max	No, he _____ . And where _____ you? Why _____ you there?
Kim	Oh, … I _____ go because I _____ at Mark's party! It _____ great!

T 6.6 Listen and check. Listen for the pronunciation of *was* and *were*. Practice with a partner.

Four geniuses!

3 Who are the people in the photographs?

4 Look at these sentences.

I was born in Brooklyn, New York, in 1973.
I could read when I was four. My sister couldn't read until she was seven.

Match lines in **A**, **B**, and **C** and make similar sentences about the four people and about you.

A	B	C
Mozart / born in	the United States / 1975	paint / one
Picasso / born in	Germany / 1879	play golf / three
Tiger Woods / born in	Austria / 1756	play the piano / three
Einstein / born in	Spain / 1881	couldn't speak / eight

5 Ask and answer questions with a partner about these people.

When was Mozart born?

Where was he born?

How old was he when he could … ?

6 Work in groups. Ask and answer questions about you.
1. Where were you born?
2. When were you born?
3. How old were you when you could … ?
   - walk
   - talk
   - read
   - swim
   - ride a bike
   - use a computer
   - speak a foreign language

Check it

7 Put a check (✓) next to the correct sentence.
1. ☐ I don't can use a computer.
   ☐ I can't use a computer.
2. ☐ Was they at the party?
   ☐ Were they at the party?
3. ☐ I'm sorry. I can't go to the party.
   ☐ I'm sorry. I no can go to the party.
4. ☐ She was no at home.
   ☐ She wasn't at home.
5. ☐ He could play chess when he was five.
   ☐ He can play chess when he was five.
6. ☐ I can to speak English very well.
   ☐ I can speak English very well.

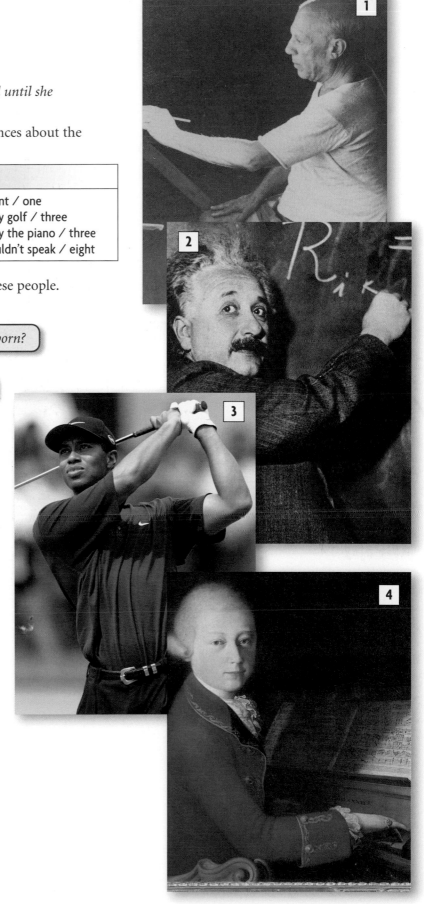

READING AND SPEAKING
Super kids

1 Look at the children in the photographs. How old are they? What can they do?

2 Work in two groups.

    Group A Read about "The New Picasso."
    Group B Read about "The New Mozart."

3 Answer the questions about Alexandra or Wesley.

  1. How old is she/he?
  2. Why is she/he special?
  3. Where was she/he born?
  4. Where does she/he live now?
  5. Who does she/he live with?
  6. Does she/he go to school?
  7. What could she/he do when she/he was very young?
  8. Does she/he have much free time?
  9. Where was she/he last year?

4 Find a partner from the other group. Tell your partner about your child, using your answers.

5 What is the same about Alexandra and Wesley? What is different? Discuss with your partner.

> *They are both geniuses.*

> *Alexandra is a painter, and Wesley is a pianist.*

Role play

6 Work with a partner.

    Student A You are a journalist.
    Student B You are Alexandra or Wesley.

    Go to page 113.

The New **Mozart**

Eight-year-old **Wesley Chu** is a happy little boy, bu[t] plays serious music. He is a world-famous pianist. He ca[n] also write music. Some people call him the "New Mozar[t]." Every year he travels the world and gives concerts. Last [year] he was in London, Hong Kong, and Rome. "It's fun," he sa[ys].

Wesley was born in Calgary, Alberta, Canada, where [he] still lives with his parents and his two sisters. He goes t[o] school five days a week and practices piano for two hou[rs a] day. Wesley could play the piano when he was only thre[e] years old. He could write music before he could write th[e] alphabet. He wrote his first piece of music when he was [...].

Wesley isn't exactly like Mozart. He doesn't just play [the] piano and write music. He also likes watching TV, playing video games, and playing with Legos. He says, "I want to [be] lots of things—an astronaut, a scientist, a cartoonist, an[d a] pianist, of course!"

The New **Picasso**

Alexandra Nechita is 13 and she is called "The New Picasso." She paints large pictures in a cubist style and sells them for between $10,000 and $80,000.

She was born in Romania, but now she lives in Los Angeles with her family. She could paint very well when she was only four, but her parents couldn't understand her pictures. Alexandra says, "I paint how I feel, sometimes I'm happy and sometimes sad. I can't stop painting." Every day after school she does her homework, plays with her little brother, then paints for two or three hours until bedtime.

Alexandra doesn't spend her money, she saves it: "We were very poor when we were first in America. We couldn't buy many things, but now I can buy a big house for my family and we can travel the world. Last year we were in London, Paris, and Rome. It was fantastic!"

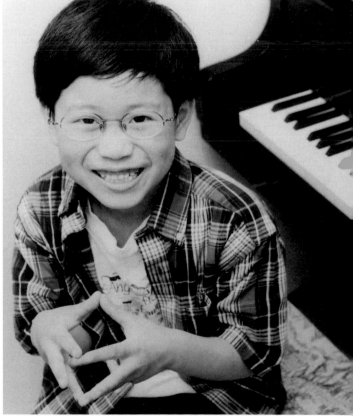

VOCABULARY AND PRONUNCIATION
Words that sound the same

1 Look at the sentences. What do you notice about these words?

I have a black **eye**.
No, he doesn't **know** the answer.

2 Find the words in **B** that have the same pronunciation as the words in **A**.

A

write   wear
hear   there   hour
    eye
see   for
by   too
    son
know

B

sun
four   I
our   sea   where
here
buy   right
    no
two   their

3 Correct the two spelling mistakes in each sentence.

hear   *see*
1. I can ~~here~~ you, but I can't ~~sea~~ you.
2. Their are three bedrooms in hour house.
3. I don't no wear Jill lives.
4. My sun lives near the see.
5. Don't where that hat, by a new one!
6. Know, eye can't come to your party.
7. You were write. Sally and Peter can't come four dinner.
8. There daughter could right when she was three.
9. I no my answers are write.

4 Look at the word and the phonetic symbols. Write the other word with the same pronunciation.

1. /noʊ/   know   _____
2. /sʌn/   son   _____
3. /tu/   too   _____
4. /raɪt/   right   _____
5. /hɪr/   here   _____
6. /wɛr/   wear   _____

EVERYDAY ENGLISH
On the phone

1 When you don't know someone's telephone number, you can call International Directory Assistance. Here are the names and addresses of some people you want to call.

WILSON ASSOCIATES
Nancy Wilson
302 Erindale Road
PERTH 6034
Australia
Tel: _____
e-mail:
n.wilson@connect.com.au

GENKI DESIGNS
VANCOUVER
Noriko Tanaka
85 Robson Street
Vancouver, British Columbia V6G 1B9
Canada
Tel: _____   Fax: _____
e-mail: tanaka@hotmall.com

35 Market Street
Atlanta, GA 30324
USA
e-mail: PWPaulson@yoohoo.com
Tel: _____
Fax: _____
Phillip W. Paulson

T 6.7 Listen to the operator and answer her questions. Get Nancy's telephone number.

Operator International Directory Assistance. Which country, please?
You   Australia   .
Operator And the city?
You   _____ .
Operator Can I have the last name, please?
You   _____ .
Operator And the first name?
You   _____ .
Operator What's the address?
You   _____ .
Recorded message The number is _____ .

2 Work with a partner. Ask and answer questions to get the phone and fax numbers of Noriko and Phillip.
Student A Go to page 114.
Student B Go to page 123.

3 Read the lines below. They are all from telephone conversations.
What do you think the lines before and/or after are? Discuss with a partner.

1. This is Gina.
2. Can I take a message?
3. Great! See you on Sunday at ten. Bye!
4. That's OK. Maybe next time. Bye!
5. No, it isn't. Hold on… I'll get her.
6. I'll call again later.
7. There's a party at my house on Saturday. Can you come?
8. Can I speak to the manager, please?

> **!** I'll = I will
> will = an offer or promise
> I'll help you

4 Complete each conversation with a line from Exercise 3.

1. **A** Hello.
   B Hello. Can I speak to Gina, please?
   A _____ .
   B Oh! Hi, Gina. This is Pat. Is Sunday still OK for tennis?
   A Yes, that's fine.
   B _____ .
   A Bye!

2. **A** Hello.
   B Hello. Is this Liz?
   A _____ .
   C Hello, this is Liz.
   B Hi, Liz. It's Tom. Listen!
   _____ .
   C Oh, I'm sorry, but I can't. It's my sister's wedding.
   B _____ !
   C Bye!

3. **A** Good morning. Bank One. How can I help you?
   B Good morning.
   _____ .
   A I'm afraid Mr. Smith isn't in his office at the moment.
   _____ ?
   B No, that's OK.
   _____ .
   A All right. Good-bye.
   B Good-bye.

T 6.8 Listen and check. Practice the conversations.

Make similar conversations with your partner.

7 Then and now

STARTER ▶ When were your grandparents and great grandparents born? Where were they born? Do you know all their names? What were their jobs? If you know, tell the class.

WHEN I WAS YOUNG
Past Simple – regular verbs

1 **T 7.1** Read and listen to Mattie Smith's life now. Complete Text A with the verbs you hear.

B

Mattie was never at school. She lived with her mother and four sisters. She started work when she was eight. She worked in the cotton fields from morning until night. She couldn't read or write but she could think, and she created poems in her head.

A

Mattie Smith is 91 years old. She _lives_ alone in Atlanta, Georgia. She _____ her day at 7:30. First she _____ a bath, next she _____ the house, and then she _____ outside on her front porch and _____ about her past life. Then she _____ poems about it.

2 **T 7.2** Read and listen to Text B about Mattie's life a long time ago.

GRAMMAR SPOT

1 Find examples of the past of *is* and *can* in Text B.

2 Complete the sentence with *live* in the correct form.
Now she _____ alone, but when she was a child she _____ with her mother and sisters.

3 Find the Past Simple of *start, work,* and *create* in Text B. How do we form the Past Simple of regular verbs?

▶▶ **Grammar Reference 7.1 p. 139**

3 **T 7.3** What is the past form of these verbs? Listen and practice saying them.

> look   work   love   learn   earn   marry   die   hate   want

4 **T 7.4** Read and listen to Mattie talking about her past life. Complete the text, using the Past Simple form of the verbs in Exercise 3.

"I __worked__ all day, from morning until night. Twelve hours in the cotton fields, and I only _____ $4 a day. I sure _____ that job, but I _____ the poems in my head. I really _____ to learn to read and write.

"When I was sixteen I _____ Hubert, and soon there were six children, five sons, then a daughter, Lily. Hubert _____ just before she was born. That was sixty-five years ago. So I _____ after my family alone.

"There was no time for learning, but my children, they all _____ to read and write. That was important to me. And when did I learn to read and write? I didn't learn until I was 86, and now I have 3 books of poems."

'THE KODAK SHOP, PUBL.'

GRAMMAR SPOT

1 Find a question and a negative in the last part of the text about Mattie.

2 Look at these questions.
   Where **does** she live now?
   Where **did** she live in 1950?
   Did is the past of *do* and *does*. We use *did* to form a question in the Past Simple.

3 We use *didn't* (= *did not*) to form the negative.
   She **didn't** learn to read until she was 86.

▶▶ **Grammar Reference 7.2 p. 139**

5 Complete the questions about Mattie. Practice the questions and answers with a partner.

1. When __did__ she __start__ to work?   When she was eight years old.
2. Where _____ she _____ ?   In the cotton fields.
3. Who _____ she _____ with?   Her mother and sisters.
4. How many hours _____ she _____ ?   Twelve hours a day.
5. How much _____ she _____ ?   Four dollars a day.
6. Who _____ she _____ ?   Hubert.
7. When _____ Hubert _____ ?   Sixty-five years ago.
8. When _____ she _____ to read?   She didn't learn until she was 86.

T 7.5 Listen and check. Practice the questions and answers with a partner.

PRACTICE

Talking about you

1 Complete the sentences with *did*, *was*, or *were*.

1. Where __were__ you born? Where _____ your mother born?
2. When _____ you start school?
3. When _____ you learn to read and write?
4. Who _____ your first teacher?
5. What _____ your favorite subject?
6. Where _____ you live when you _____ a child?
7. _____ you live in a house or an apartment?

2 Stand up! Ask two or three students the questions in Exercise 1.

3 Tell the class some of the information you learned.

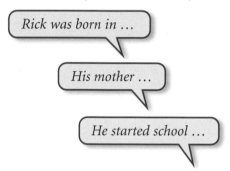

Rick was born in …

His mother …

He started school …

Pronunciation

4 **T 7.6** The *-ed* ending of regular verbs has three different pronunciations. Listen to the examples. Then put the verbs you hear in the correct column.

/t/	/d/	/ɪd/
• worked	• lived	• started
•	•	•
•	•	•
•	•	

THE END OF THE 20TH CENTURY
Irregular verbs

1 Look at the list of irregular verbs on page 152. Write the Past Simple form of the verbs in the box. Which two verbs *aren't* irregular?

have _____	fight _____	study _____	become _____
leave _____	get _____	buy _____	meet _____
win _____	lose _____	go (2x) _____	die _____

2 **T 7.7** Listen and repeat.

3 **T 7.8** How old were you in 2000? Steve was twenty-four in the year 2000. Listen to him and complete the sentences.

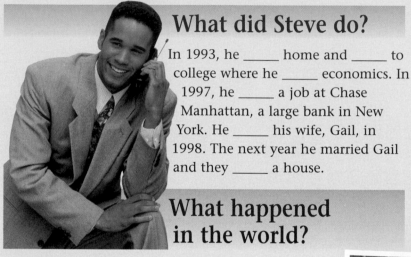

What did Steve do?

In 1993, he _____ home and _____ to college where he _____ economics. In 1997, he _____ a job at Chase Manhattan, a large bank in New York. He _____ his wife, Gail, in 1998. The next year he married Gail and they _____ a house.

What happened in the world?

Sports
Brazil _____ the soccer World Cup in 1994, but they _____ in 1998 to France.

Politics
The United States _____ in the Gulf War in 1991. Bill Clinton _____ president in 1992. He was president for eight years. We _____ problems with the presidential election in 2000.

Famous people
Princess Diana _____ in a car crash in Paris in 1997. Millions of people _____ to London for her funeral.

Listen again and check.

4 Work with a partner. Ask and answer questions about Steve.

1. When/Steve/leave home?
2. What/study at college?
3. When/a job with Chase Manhattan Bank?
4. When/meet Gail?
5. What/Gail and Steve do in 1999?

5 What did *you* do in the last years of the 20th century? What can you remember? Write about it. Tell the class.

PRACTICE

When did it happen?

1 Work in small groups. What important dates in the 20th century can you remember? What happened in the world? What happened in your country? Make a list of events. Then make questions to ask the other groups.

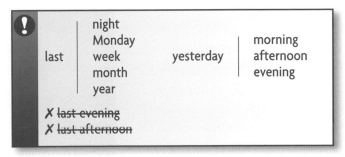

> *When did the first person walk on the moon?*

> *When did France win the World Cup?*

What did you do?

2 Look at these phrases.

!				
last	night Monday week month year	yesterday	morning afternoon evening

✗ ~~last evening~~
✗ ~~last afternoon~~

3 Work with a partner. Ask and answer questions with *When did you last … ?* Ask another question for more information.

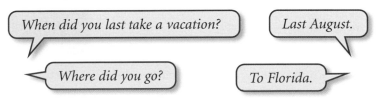

> *When did you last take a vacation?*

> *Last August.*

> *Where did you go?*

> *To Florida.*

- take a vacation
- watch a video
- go shopping
- give someone a kiss
- take a photograph
- go to a party
- lose something
- write a letter
- get a present
- have dinner in a restaurant

Tell the class some things you learned about your partner.

> *Yukio took a vacation last August and she went to Italy.*

Check it

4 Put a check (✓) next to the correct sentence.

1. ☐ He bought some new shoes.
   ☐ He buyed some new shoes.
2. ☐ Where did you go yesterday?
   ☐ Where you went yesterday?
3. ☐ You see Jane last week?
   ☐ Did you see Jane last week?
4. ☐ Did she get the job?
   ☐ Did she got the job?
5. ☐ I went out yesterday night.
   ☐ I went out last night.
6. ☐ He studied French at college.
   ☐ He studyed French at college.
7. ☐ What had you for breakfast?
   ☐ What did you have for breakfast?
8. ☐ I was in New York the last week.
   ☐ I was in New York last week.

READING AND SPEAKING
Two famous firsts

1 Translate these words.

Nouns					
freedom	lawyer	politician	prison	slaves	widow
Verbs					
fight	grow	own	retire		

2 Look at the photographs and complete the sentences.

George Washington was the first _____ .

Nelson Mandela was the first _____ .

What else do you know about these people?

3 Work in two groups.

Group A Read about George Washington.
Group B Read about Nelson Mandela.

4 Are the sentences true (✔) or false (✗) about your person? Correct the false sentences.

1. He was the first president of his country.
2. He was in prison for 28 years.
3. His father died when he was young.
4. He fought in two wars.
5. He married a widow.
6. He had two daughters.
7. He was president for eight years.
8. He retired from politics when he was 80.

5 Find a partner from the other group. Compare George Washington and Nelson Mandela, using your answers.

6 Complete the questions about the other person. Then ask and answer them with your partner.

About George Washington
1. How many jobs did he … ?
2. When did he … president?
3. What did he … doing in his free time?
4. Did George and Martha have any … ?
5. What did he … to build?
6. How long … he president?

About Nelson Mandela
7. What … his father's job? ·
8. When did he … Winnie?
9. How many children did they … ?
10. When … he go to prison?
11. When did he … the Nobel Prize?
12. How long … he president?

What do you think?

Who were famous leaders in your country?
What did they do?

Two Famous Firsts

George Washington (1732–1799)

He was the first president of the United States. He became president in 1789, eight years after the American War of Independence.

His early life

George was born in Virginia. His family owned a big farm and had slaves. George didn't have much education. During his life he had three jobs: he was a farmer, a soldier, and a politician. He loved the life of a farmer. He grew tobacco and owned horses. He worked hard but he also liked dancing and going to the theater. In 1759 he married a widow called Martha Custis. They were happy together, but didn't have any children.

His later life

He was Commander-in-Chief of the army and fought the British in the War of Independence. When the war ended in 1783 he was happy to go back to the farm, but his country wanted him to be president. Finally, in 1789, he became president, and gave his name to the new capital city. He started the building of the White House, but he never lived in it. By 1797 he was tired of politics. He went back to his farm and died there two years later.

Nelson Mandela (1918–)

He was the first black president of South Africa. He became president in 1994.

His early life

Nelson was born in Qunu, a small village in South Africa. His father was an important man in the village, but he died when Nelson was still young. Nelson worked hard and went to a university where he studied history and languages. At the university he became interested in politics and joined the African National Congress. Nelson studied law and became a lawyer in 1952. In 1958, he married Winnie Mandela. They had two daughters.

His later life

Nelson became a leader in the African National Congress which fought against the all-white South African government. In 1962 he went to prison. He finally left prison in 1990, and in 1993 he won the Nobel Peace Prize. He became the first black president of South Africa in 1994. He retired from politics in 1999 at the age of 80 and went back to Qunu.

VOCABULARY AND PRONUNCIATION
Spelling and silent letters

1 There are many silent letters in English words. Here are some words from the reading texts on page 53.

wido**w**	/ˈwɪdoʊ/
b**u**ilding	/ˈbɪldɪŋ/
fou**gh**t	/fɔt/
white	/waɪt/

T 7.9 Listen and practice saying them.

2 **T 7.10** Listen and cross out the silent letters in these words.

1. wa~~l~~k
2. listen
3. know
4. write
5. eight
6. buy
7. hour
8. island
9. could
10. daughter

Practice saying the words.

3 Look at the phonetic spelling of these words from Exercise 2. Write the words.

1. /wɔk/   **walk**
2. /baɪ/   _____
3. /ˈlɪsən/   _____
4. /raɪt/   _____
5. /ˈdɔtər/   _____
6. /noʊ/   _____

4 **T 7.11** Listen and write the words. They all have silent letters.

1. /bɔt/   **bought**
2. /kʊd/   _____
3. /naɪt/   _____
4. /ˈænsər/   _____
5. /ˈaɪlənd/   _____
6. /ˈkrɪsməs/   _____

Practice saying the words.

5 Read these sentences aloud.

1. He bought his daughter eight, white horses for Christmas.
2. I know you know the answer.
3. They walked and talked for hours and hours.

T 7.12 Listen and check.

EVERYDAY ENGLISH
Special occasions

1 Look at the list of days. Which are special? Match the special days with the pictures. Do you have the same customs in your country?

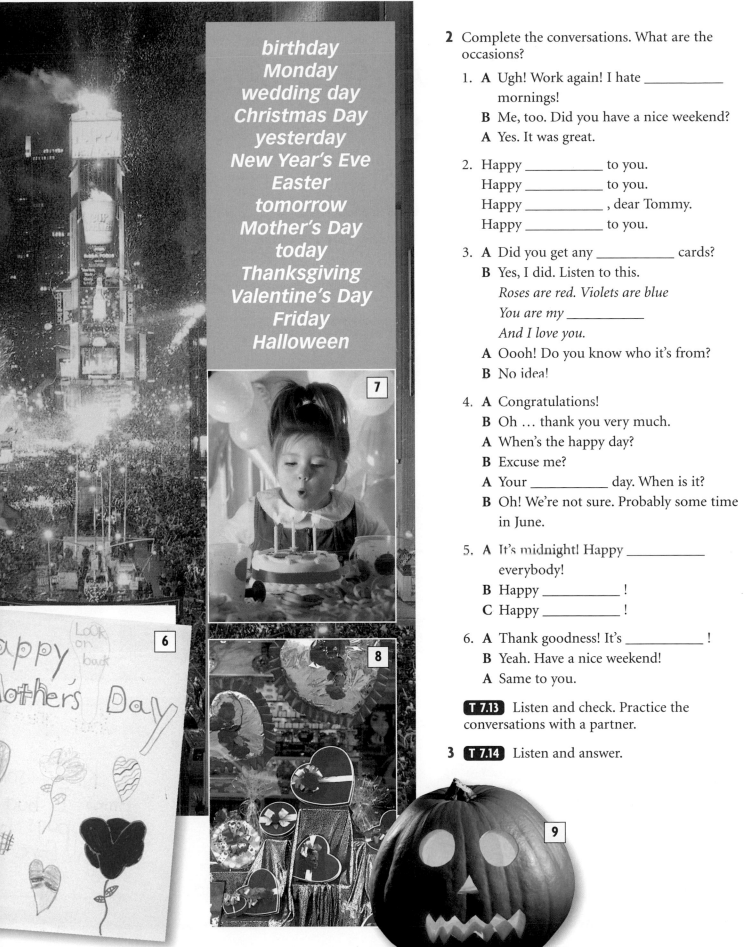

birthday
Monday
wedding day
Christmas Day
yesterday
New Year's Eve
Easter
tomorrow
Mother's Day
today
Thanksgiving
Valentine's Day
Friday
Halloween

2 Complete the conversations. What are the occasions?

1. **A** Ugh! Work again! I hate _____ mornings!
   B Me, too. Did you have a nice weekend?
   A Yes. It was great.

2. Happy _____ to you.
   Happy _____ to you.
   Happy _____ , dear Tommy.
   Happy _____ to you.

3. **A** Did you get any _____ cards?
   B Yes, I did. Listen to this.
      Roses are red. Violets are blue
      You are my _____
      And I love you.
   A Oooh! Do you know who it's from?
   B No idea!

4. **A** Congratulations!
   B Oh … thank you very much.
   A When's the happy day?
   B Excuse me?
   A Your _____ day. When is it?
   B Oh! We're not sure. Probably some time in June.

5. **A** It's midnight! Happy _____ everybody!
   B Happy _____ !
   C Happy _____ !

6. **A** Thank goodness! It's _____ !
   B Yeah. Have a nice weekend!
   A Same to you.

T 7.13 Listen and check. Practice the conversations with a partner.

3 **T 7.14** Listen and answer.

8 How long ago?

Past Simple 2 – negatives/*ago* • Which word is different? • What's the date?

Say the Past Simple of these verbs. Most of them are irregular.

| eat | drink | drive | fly | listen to | make | ride | take | watch | wear |

FAMOUS INVENTIONS
Past Simple negatives/*ago*

1 Match the verbs from the Starter to the photographs.

| 1 | drink | Coca-Cola |

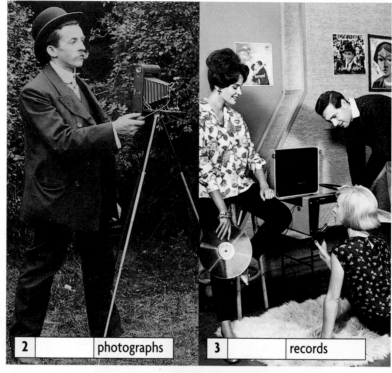

| 2 | | photographs |

| 3 | | records |

| 4 | | planes |

| 5 | | jeans |

10	bicycles

2 Work in groups. What year was it one hundred years ago? Ask and answer questions about the things in the pictures. What did people do? What didn't they do?

> *Did people drive cars one hundred years ago?*

> *Yes, I think they did.*

> *I'm not sure.*

> *No, they didn't.*

3 Tell the class the things you think people did and didn't do.

> *We think people drove cars, but they didn't watch TV.*

Getting Information

4 Work with a partner. When were the things in Exercise 1 invented?

Student A Go to page 115.
Student B Go to page 116.

6	hamburgers

7	cars

8	phone calls

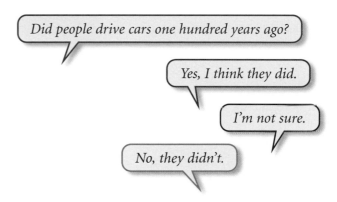

9	television

GRAMMAR SPOT

Write the Past Simple forms.

Present Simple	Past Simple
I live in Seattle.	<u>I lived in Seattle.</u>
He lives in Seattle.	
Do you live in Seattle?	
Does she live in Seattle?	
I don't live in Seattle.	
He doesn't live in Seattle.	

▶▶ **Grammar Reference 8.1 and 8.2 p. 139**

PRACTICE

Three inventors

1 [T 8.1] The dates in the texts are *all* incorrect.
Read and listen, and correct the dates.

They didn't make the first jeans in 1923. They made them in 1873.

Jeans

Two Americans, Jacob Davis and **Levi Strauss,** made the first jeans in 1923. Davis bought cloth from Levi's shop. He told Levi that he had a special way to make strong clothing for workmen. The first jeans were blue. In 1965 jeans became fashionable for women after they saw them in *Vogue* magazine. In the 1990s, Calvin Klein earned $12.5 million a week from jeans.

Television

A Scotsman, **John Logie Baird,** transmitted the first television picture on November 25, 1905. The first thing on television was a boy who worked in the office next to Baird's workroom in London. In 1929 Baird sent pictures from London to Glasgow. In 1940 he sent pictures to New York, and also produced the first color TV pictures.

Aspirin

Felix Hofman, a 29-year-old chemist who worked for the German company Bayer, invented the drug Aspirin in April 1879. He gave the first aspirin to his father for his arthritis. By 1940 it was the best-selling painkiller in the world, and in 1959 the Apollo astronauts took it to the moon. The Spanish philosopher José Ortega y Gasset called the 20th century "The Age of Aspirin."

2 Make these sentences negative. Then give the correct answers.

1. Two Germans made the first blue jeans.
   Two Germans didn't make the first jeans. Two Americans made them.
2. Davis sold cloth in Levi's shop.
3. Women saw pictures of jeans in *She* magazine.

4. Baird sent pictures from London to Paris.
5. Felix Hofman gave the first aspirin to his mother.
6. A Spanish philosopher called the 19th century "The Age of Aspirin."

[T 8.2] Listen and check. Practice the stress and intonation.

Did you know that?

3 [T 8.3] Read and listen to the conversations. Then listen and repeat.

A Did you know that Marco Polo brought spaghetti back from China?
B Really? That's incredible!
A Well, it's true!

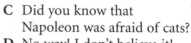

C Did you know that Napoleon was afraid of cats?
D No way! I don't believe it!
C Well, it's true!

4 Work with a partner. Look at the lists of more incredible information. Have similar conversations.

Student A Go to page 117.
Student B Go to page 118.

Time expressions

5 Make correct time expressions.

	seven o'clock
	the morning
	Saturday
in	Sunday evening
on	night
at	September
	weekends
	summer
	1994
	the twentieth century

6 Work with a partner. Ask and answer questions with *When ... ?* Use a time expression and *ago* in the answer.

When did you get up?

At seven o'clock, three hours ago.

When did this class start?

In September, two months ago.

When did . . . ?

• you get up?
• you have breakfast?
• you arrive at school?
• you start learning English?
• you start at this school?
• this semester start?
• you last use a computer?
• you learn to ride a bicycle?
• your parents get married?
• you last eat a hamburger?
• you last have a coffee break?

7 Tell the class about your day so far. Begin like this.

I got up at seven o'clock, had breakfast, and left the house at ...

VOCABULARY AND PRONUNCIATION
Which word is different?

1 Which word is different? Why?

1. orange   apple   ~~chicken~~   banana
   Chicken is different because it isn't a fruit.
2. hamburger   sandwich   pizza   recipe
3. television   dishwasher   vacuum cleaner   washing machine
4. wrote   kissed   threw   found
5. fax   e-mail   CD player   cell phone
6. brown   green   delicious   blue
7. face   eye   mouth   leg
8. talk   speak   chat   laugh
9. century   clock   season   month
10. funny   shy   nervous   worried
11. fall in love   get married   get engaged   go to a party

2 Match these words from Exercise 1 with their phonetic spelling. Practice saying the words.

banana	clock	delicious	funny
green	kissed	recipe	worried

1. /ˈrɛsəpi/   <u>recipe</u>
2. /ɡrin/   _____
3. /klɑk/   _____
4. /bəˈnænə/   _____
5. /ˈfʌni/   _____
6. /ˈwərid/   _____
7. /dɪˈlɪʃəs/   _____
8. /kɪst/   _____

T 8.4 Listen and check.

3 Complete the sentences with a word from Exercise 1.

1. **A** Why didn't you _____ at my joke?
   B Because it wasn't very _____ . That's why!
2. **A** Hello. Hello. I can't hear you. Who is it?
   B It's me Jonathan ... JONATHAN! I'm on my _____ .
   A Oh, Jonathan! Hi! Sorry, I can't _____ now. I'm in a hurry.
3. **A** Good luck on your exams!
   B Oh, thank you. I always get so _____ before exams.
4. **A** Mmmmm! Did you make this chocolate cake?
   B I did. Do you like it?
   A Like it? I love it. It's _____ . Can I have the _____ ?
5. **A** Come on, Tommy. Say hello to your Aunt Mavis. Don't be _____ .
   B Hello, Aunt Mavis.

T 8.5 Listen and check. Practice the conversations.

LISTENING AND SPEAKING
How did you two meet?

1 Put the sentences in the correct order. Read the story aloud. There is more than one answer!

____ They got married.   ____ They talked for a long time.

____ They fell in love.   ____ They had two children.

_1_ Wilma and Carl met at a party. ____ They kissed.

____ He invited her to meet his parents. ____ They got engaged.

2 Look at the four people and discuss the questions.
The people are:
- **Vince Banks** from Anchorage, Alaska
- **Marie Blanc** from Montreal, Quebec, Canada
- **Chris Atlas** from San Francisco, California
- **Yuko Ikeda** from Sendai, Japan

1. Who do you think is who? Why?
2. Who do you think are husband and wife? Why?
3. How do you think they met?

3 Read the introductions to the stories of how they met. What do you think happened next?

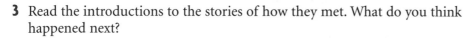

LOVE ON THE INTERNET
Nowadays love on the Internet is big business. Millions try to find true love there every day. Chris Atlas from San Francisco, California, and Marie Blanc from Montreal, Quebec, Canada, looked for love that way …

LOVE IN A BOTTLE
Fisherman Vince Banks from Anchorage, Alaska, couldn't find a wife, so he wrote a letter, put it in a bottle, and threw it into the ocean. Ten years later and eight thousand kilometers away in Japan, Yuko Ikeda found the bottle on the beach …

4 **T 8.6** Now listen to them talking. Were your ideas correct?

5 Answer the questions about Chris and Marie, and Vince and Yuko.

1. When did they meet?
2. Why does Marie like to chat on the Internet?
3. Where was Vince's letter? What did it say?
4. Why couldn't Yuko read the letter?
5. Do both couples have children?
6. Who says these sentences? Write **C**, **M**, **V**, or **Y**.

   a. ____ I'm really shy.
   ____ I was very shy.
   b. ____ I find it difficult to talk to people face-to-face.
   ____ I flew to the U.S. and we met face-to-face.
   c. ____ I stood on something.
   ____ I stood there with some flowers.
   d. ____ We chatted on the Internet for a year.
   ____ We wrote every week for six months.

Speaking

6 Imagine you are one of the people. Tell the story of how you met your husband/wife.

7 Look at the questions. Tell a partner about you and your family.

1. Are you married or do you have a girlfriend/boyfriend? How did you meet?
2. When did your parents or grandparents meet? Where? How?

EVERYDAY ENGLISH
What's the date?

1 Write the correct word next to the numbers.

| fourth | twelfth | sixth | twentieth | second | thirtieth | thirteenth |
| thirty-first | fifth | seventeenth | tenth | sixteenth | first | third | twenty-first |

1st	**first**	6th	_____	17th	_____
2nd	_____	10th	_____	20th	_____
3rd	_____	12th	_____	21st	_____
4th	_____	13th	_____	30th	_____
5th	_____	16th	_____	31st	_____

T 8.7 Listen and practice saying the ordinals.

2 Ask and answer questions with a partner about the months of the year.

> *Which is the first month?*

> *January.*

> ❗ We write: 4/3/99 or April 3, 1999
> We say: "April third, nineteen ninety-nine."
> Notice how we say these years:
> 1900 nineteen hundred
> 1905 nineteen oh five
> 2001 two thousand one

3 Practice saying these dates:

| April 1 | March 2 | September 17 | November 19 | June 23 |
| 2/29/76 | 12/19/83 | 10/3/99 | 5/31/2000 | 7/15/2004 |

T 8.8 Listen and check.

4 **T 8.9** Listen and write the dates you hear.

1. **January 4**   3. _____   5. _____
2. _____   4. _____   6. _____

5 Ask and answer the questions with your partner.

1. What is the date today?
2. When did this class start? When does it end?
3. When is Christmas Day?
4. When is Valentine's Day?
5. When is Mother's Day this year?
6. When is Independence Day in the United States?
7. What century is it now?
8. What are the dates of public holidays in your country?
9. When were you born?
10. When is your birthday?

9 Food you like!

Count and noncount nouns · *I like/I'd like* · *much/many* · Food · Polite requests

STARTER What's your favorite · fruit? · vegetable? · drink?

Write your answers. Compare them with a partner, then with the class.

FOOD AND DRINK

Count and noncount nouns

1 Match the food and drink with the pictures.

A		B	
_15_	coffee	___	apples
___	tea	___	oranges
___	wine	___	bananas
___	soda	___	strawberries
___	apple juice	___	peas
___	spaghetti	___	carrots
___	yogurt	___	tomatoes
___	pizza	___	cookies
___	cheese	___	hamburgers
___	chocolate	___	french fries

GRAMMAR SPOT

1 Which list in Exercise 1 has plural nouns, **A** or **B**?

2 Look at the pairs of sentences. What is the difference?

A	**B**
Chocolate **is** delicious.	Strawberries **are** delicious.
Apple juice **is** good for you.	Apples **are** good for you.

3 Can we count apple juice? Can we count apples?

▶▶ **Grammar Reference 9.1 p. 140**

2 **T 9.1** Listen to Donna and Tom talking about what they like and don't like. Put a check (✔) next to the food and drink in Exercise 1 that they both like.

Who says these things? Write *D* or *T*.

Tom   Donna

_T_ I don't like coffee, but I like tea.
___ I like apple juice. It's delicious.
___ I really like peas and carrots.
___ I don't like tomatoes very much.
___ I don't like cheese at all.

3 Talk about the items in Exercise 1 with a partner. What do you like? What do you *really* like? What *don't* you like?

I like . . . and *I'd like . . .*

1 **T 9.2** Read and listen to the conversation.

A Would you like some tea or coffee?
B I'd like a cold drink, please, if that's OK.
A Of course. Would you like some orange juice?
B Yes, please. I'd love some.
A Would you like a cookie, too?
B No, thanks. Just orange juice is fine.

GRAMMAR SPOT

1 Look at the sentences.

A	**B**
Do you like tea?	Would you like some tea?
I like cookies.	I'd like a cookie. (I'd = I would)

Which sentences, **A** or **B**, mean *Do you want/I want . . .* ?

2 Look at these sentences.

I'd like some bananas. (plural noun)
I'd like some mineral water. (noncount noun)

We use *some* with both plural and noncount nouns.

3 Look at these questions.

Would you like *some* cookies?
Can I have *some* tea?
but Are there *any* cookies?
Is there *any* tea?

We use *some*, not *any*, when we request and offer things.
We use *any*, not *some*, in other questions and negatives.

▶▶ **Grammar Reference 9.2 p. 140**

2 Practice the conversation in Exercise 1 with a partner. Then have similar conversations about other food and drink.

Would you like some cheese?

No, thanks. I don't like cheese very much.

PRACTICE

a or *some*?

1 Write *a*, *an*, or *some*.

1. __a__ strawberry
2. __some__ fruit
3. _____ mushroom
4. _____ bread
5. _____ milk
6. _____ meat

7. _____ apple
8. _____ rice
9. _____ money
10. _____ dollar
11. _____ notebook
12. _____ homework

2 Write *a*, *an*, or *some*.

1. _____ egg

2. _____ eggs

3. _____ cookie

4. _____ cookies

5. _____ coffee

6. _____ coffee

7. _____ ice cream

8. _____ ice cream

Questions and answers

3 Choose *Would/Do you like … ?* or *I/I'd like …* to complete the conversations.

1. A ☑ Would you like | a cigarette?
   ☐ Do you like |
   B No, thanks. I don't smoke.

2. A ☐ Do you like | your teacher?
   ☐ Would you like |
   B Yes. She's very nice.

3. A ☐ Do you like | a drink?
   ☐ Would you like |
   B Yes. I'd like a soda, please.

4. A Can I help you?
   B ☐ Yes. I like | a book of stamps, please.
   ☐ Yes. I'd like |

5. A What sports do you like?
   B ☐ Well, I'd like | swimming very much.
   ☐ Well, I like |

6. A Excuse me, are you ready to order?
   B ☐ Yes. I like | a hamburger, please.
   ☐ Yes. I'd like |

T 9.3 Listen and check. Practice the conversations with a partner.

4 **T 9.4** Listen to the questions and choose the correct answers.

1. ☐ I like all kinds of fruit.
   ☐ Yes. I'd like some fruit, please.

2. ☐ I'd like a book by John Grisham.
   ☐ I like books by John Grisham.

3. ☐ I'd like a new bike.
   ☐ I like riding my bike.

4. ☐ I'd like a cat but not a dog.
   ☐ I like cats, but I don't like dogs.

5. ☐ I like French wine, especially red wine.
   ☐ We'd like a bottle of French red wine, please.

6. ☐ No, thanks. I don't like strawberries.
   ☐ I'd like some ice cream, please.

T 9.5 Listen and check. Practice the conversations with your partner.

GOING SHOPPING
some/any, much/many

1 What is there in Mrs. Bloom's store?
Talk about the picture. Use
some/any, and *not much/not many*.

> There's some bread.

> There aren't any carrots.

> There isn't much coffee.

> There aren't many eggs.

2 Ask and answer questions about what
there is in the store with a partner.

> Are there any eggs?

> Yes, there are some,
> but there aren't many.

> Is there any coffee?

> Yes, there is some, but there isn't much.

3 **T 9.6** Look at Barry's shopping list.
Listen and put a check (✓) next to the
things he buys. Why doesn't he buy other
things?

THINGS TO BUY

Orange juice Cheese Apples
Milk   Pizza
Coffee   Bread

PRACTICE

much or many?

1 Complete the questions using *much* or *many*.

1. How __many__ people are there in the room?
2. How _____ money do you have in your pocket?
3. How _____ cups of coffee do you drink each day?
4. How _____ gas is there in the car?
5. How _____ apples do you want?
6. How _____ wine do we have?

2 Choose an answer for each question in Exercise 1.

a. A kilo.
b. Two bottles—one red and one white.
c. Three.
d. Only fifty cents.
e. Twenty. Nine men and eleven women.
f. The tank is full.

Check it

3 Correct the sentences.

1. How ~~much~~ apples do you want?   ✗
   How many apples do you want?
2. I don't like an ice cream.
3. Can I have a bread, please?
4. I'm hungry. I like a sandwich.
5. I don't have many milk left.
6. I'd like some fruits, please.
7. How many money do you have?
8. We have lot of homework today.

Role play

4 Work with a partner. Make a shopping list and role-play conversations between Mrs. Bloom and a customer.

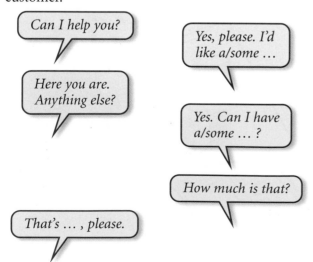

Can I help you?

Here you are. Anything else?

Yes, please. I'd like a/some …

Yes. Can I have a/some … ?

How much is that?

That's … , please.

READING AND SPEAKING
Food around the world

1 Which food and drink comes from your country? What foreign food and drink is popular in your country?

2 Can you identify any places or nationalities in the photographs? What else can you see?

3 Read the text. Write the correct question heading for each paragraph.
WHERE DOES OUR FOOD COME FROM?
WHAT DO WE EAT?
HOW DO WE EAT?

4 Answer the questions.

1. When did human history start? Was it about 10,000 years ago or was it about 1 million years ago?
2. Do they eat much rice in the south of China?
3. Why do the Japanese and Taiwanese eat a lot of fish?
4. Why don't people living in the middle of the United States eat much fish?
5. How many courses are there in China?
6. How do people eat in the Middle East?
7. Why can we eat strawberries at any time of the year?

Speaking

5 Work in small groups and discuss these questions about your country.

1. What is a typical breakfast?
2. What does your family have for breakfast?
3. Is lunch or dinner the main meal of the day?
4. What is a typical main meal?

Writing

6 Write a paragraph about meals in your country.

FOOD AROUND THE WORLD

For 99 percent of human history, people took their food from the world around them. They ate all that they could find, and then moved on. Then about 10,000 years ago, or for 1 percent of human history, people learned to farm the land and control their environment.

The kind of food we eat depends on which part of the world we live in, or which part of our country we live in. For example, in the south of China they eat a lot of rice. Noodles are more common in the north. In Japan and Taiwan, people eat a lot of fish and other seafood. But in the middle of the United States, away from the sea, people don't eat so much fish. They eat more meat and chicken.

In some European countries, and at formal dinners in North America, there are two or more courses to every meal and people eat with knives and forks.

In China there is only one course—all the food is together on the table, and they eat with chopsticks. In parts of India and the Middle East people use their fingers and bread to pick up the food.

Nowadays it is possible to transport food easily from one part of the world to another. We can eat what we like, when we like, at any time of the year. Our bananas come from Central America or Africa; our rice comes from California or Thailand; our strawberries come from Chile or Mexico. Food is very big business. But people in poor countries are still hungry, and people in rich countries eat too much.

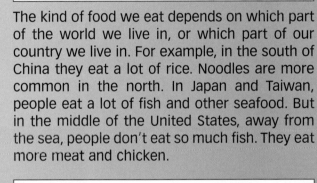

LISTENING AND SPEAKING
My favorite food

1 Look at the photographs of different food. Which do you like?

2 **T 9.7** Listen and match each person with their favorite food.

George

Mary Ann

Sally

Greg

Amy

3 Answer these questions.

Who . . . ?
- likes spicy food
- likes sweet things
- had her favorite food on vacation

- prefers vegetables
- likes food from his own country

4 What's *your* favorite food? Is it from your country or from another country?

EVERYDAY ENGLISH
Polite requests

1 What can you see in the photograph?

2 Match the questions and responses.

Would you like some more carrots?	Black, no sugar, please.
Could you pass the salt, please?	Yes, of course. I'm glad you like it.
Could I have a glass of water, please?	Do you want bottled water or tap water?
Does anybody want more dessert?	Yes, please. They're delicious.
How would you like your coffee?	Sure. Here you are.
This is delicious! Can you give me the recipe?	That's OK. We have a dishwasher.
Do you want some help with the dishes?	Yes, please. I'd love some. It's delicious.

> **!** We use *Can/Could I ...?*
> to ask for things.
> Can I have a glass of water?
> Could I have a glass of water?
>
> We use *Can/Could you ...?*
> to ask other people to do
> things for us.
> Can you give me the recipe?
> Could you pass the salt?

T 9.8 Listen and check. Practice the questions and answers with a partner.

3 Complete these requests with *Can/Could I ... ?* or *Can/Could you ... ?*

1. _____ have a cheese sandwich, please?
2. _____ tell me the time, please?
3. _____ take me to school?
4. _____ see the menu, please?
5. _____ lend me some money, please?
6. _____ help me with my homework, please?
7. _____ borrow your dictionary, please?

4 Practice the requests in Exercise 3 with a partner. Give an answer for each request.

· Can I have a cheese sandwich, please?   *Yes, of course. That's $3.50.*

T 9.9 Listen and compare your answers.

10 Bigger and better!

Comparatives and superlatives · Town and country · Directions 2

STARTER Work with a partner. Who is taller? Who is older? Tell the class.

> *I'm taller and older than Maria. She's shorter and younger than me.*

CITY LIFE/COUNTRY LIFE
Comparative adjectives

Adjective	Opposite
fast	cheap
big	slow
dirty	friendly
dangerous	clean
noisy	quiet
modern	old
unfriendly	safe
exciting	boring
expensive	small

1 Match an adjective with its opposite.
Which adjectives describe life in the city?
Which describe life in the country?

2 Make sentences comparing life in the city and country.

The city is	cheaper	than the country.
The country is	safer	than the city.
	noisier	
	dirtier	
	more expensive	
	more exciting	

3 What do you think? Tell the class.

> *I think it's safer in the country, but the city is more exciting.*

GRAMMAR SPOT

1 Complete these comparatives. What are the rules?
   I'm _____ (old) than you.
   Your class is _____ (noisy) than my class.
   Your car was _____ (expensive) than my car.

2 **T 10.1** Listen and repeat.

3 What are the comparatives of the adjectives in Exercise 1?

4 The comparatives of *good* and *bad* are irregular. What are they?
   good _____   bad _____

▶▶ **Grammar Reference 10.1 p. 141**

PRACTICE

Much more than . . .

1 Complete the conversations with the correct form of the adjectives.

1. **A** Life in the country is **slower than** city life. (slow)

   B Yes, city life is much **faster** . (fast)

2. **A** Los Angeles is _____ _____ London. (safe)

   B No, it isn't. Los Angeles is _____ _____ . (dangerous)

3. **A** Brasilia is _____ _____ São Paolo. (big)

   B No, it isn't! It's much _____ . (small)

4. **A** Taipei is _____ _____ _____ Tokyo. (expensive)

   B No, it isn't. Taipei is much _____ . (cheap)

5. **A** The buildings in Rome are _____ _____ _____ the buildings in New York. (modern)

   B No, they aren't. They're much _____ . (old)

6. **A** The subway in New York is _____ _____ the Metro in Paris. (good)

   B No! The subway is much _____ . (bad)

T 10.2 Listen and check. Practice with a partner.

2 **T 10.3** Meg moved from Los Angeles to Lakeport, a small town in northern California. Read and listen to Meg's conversation with her friend Tara. Complete it with the correct adjectives.

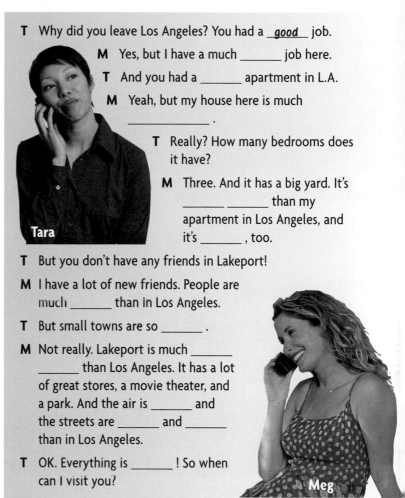

T Why did you leave Los Angeles? You had a **good** job.

M Yes, but I have a much _____ job here.

T And you had a _____ apartment in L.A.

M Yeah, but my house here is much _____ .

T Really? How many bedrooms does it have?

M Three. And it has a big yard. It's _____ _____ than my apartment in Los Angeles, and it's _____ , too.

T But you don't have any friends in Lakeport!

M I have a lot of new friends. People are much _____ than in Los Angeles.

T But small towns are so _____ .

M Not really. Lakeport is much _____ _____ than Los Angeles. It has a lot of great stores, a movie theater, and a park. And the air is _____ and the streets are _____ and _____ than in Los Angeles.

T OK. Everything is _____ ! So when can I visit you?

3 Practice the conversation with a partner.

4 Work with a partner. Compare two towns or cities that you both know. Which do you like better? Why?

THE WORLD'S BEST HOTELS
Superlative adjectives

1 Read about the three hotels.

The Plaza
New York

- 94 years old
- 812 rooms
- $350–$800 a night
- 45 minutes to Kennedy Airport
- no swimming pool

The Mandarin Oriental
Hong Kong

- 36 years old
- 542 rooms
- $450–$3,200 a night
- 30 minutes to Chek Lap Kok Airport
- swimming pool

Claridge's
London

- 100 years old
- 292 rooms
- $500–$4,000 a night
- 35 minutes to Heathrow Airport
- no swimming pool

2 Correct the false (✗) sentences. How many correct (✓) sentences are there? What do you notice about them?

1. The Mandarin Oriental is cheaper than the Plaza. ✗
   No, it isn't. It's more expensive.
2. The Plaza is the cheapest. ✓
3. Claridge's is the most expensive hotel.
4. The Mandarin Oriental is older than the Plaza.
5. Claridge's is the oldest hotel.
6. The Plaza is the biggest hotel.
7. The Mandarin Oriental is smaller than Claridge's.
8. The Plaza has a swimming pool.
9. Claridge's is closer to the airport than the Mandarin.
10. The Mandarin is the closest to the airport.
11. The Plaza is the farthest from the airport.

3 Which is the best hotel in or near *your* town? Describe it.

1 Complete these superlative sentences. What's the rule?

The Green Palace is the _____ (cheap) hotel in New York.

The Four Seasons is the _____ _____ (expensive).

2 Dictionaries often show irregular comparative and superlative forms of adjectives. Look at this:

good /gʊd/ adj. (**better**, **best**)

Complete these irregular forms:

bad /bæd/ adj. (_____ , _____)

far /fɑr/ adj. (_____ , _____)

▶▶ **Grammar Reference 10.1 p. 141**

PRACTICE

The biggest and best!

1 Complete the conversations using the superlative form of the adjective.

1. **A** That house is very big.

   B Yes, _it's the biggest house_ in town.

2. **A** Claridge's is a very expensive hotel.

   B Yes, _____ in London.

3. **A** San Francisco is a beautiful city.

   B Yes, _____ in the United States.

4. **A** New York is a very cosmopolitan city.

   B Yes, _____ in the world.

5. **A** Tom Hanks is a very popular actor.

   B Yes, _____ in the United States.

6. **A** Ms. Smith is a very funny teacher.

   B Yes, _____ in our school.

7. **A** Ana is a very intelligent student.

   B Yes, _____ in our class.

8. **A** This is a very easy exercise.

   B Yes, _____ in the book.

T 10.4 Listen and check.

2 **T 10.5** Close your books. Listen to the first line and give the answer.

Talking about your class

3 How well do you know the other students in your class? Describe them using these adjectives and others.

| tall   short   old   young   intelligent   funny |

I think Roger is the tallest in the class. He's taller than Carl.

Maria's the youngest.

I'm the most intelligent!

4 Write the name of your favorite actor. Read it to the class. Compare the people. Which actor is the most popular in your class?

Check it

5 Put a check (✓) next to the correct sentence.

1. ☐ Yesterday was more hot than today.
   ☐ Yesterday was hotter than today.

2. ☐ She's older than her brother.
   ☐ She's older that her brother.

3. ☐ I'm the most young in the class.
   ☐ I'm the youngest in the class.

4. ☐ Last week was busier than this week.
   ☐ Last week was busyer than this week.

5. ☐ My brother is the most tall in the family.
   ☐ My brother is the tallest in the family.

6. ☐ New York is the most exciting city in the world.
   ☐ New York is the most excitingest city in the world.

7. ☐ My homework is the baddest in the class.
   ☐ My homework is the worst in the class.

8. ☐ This exercise is the most difficult in the book.
   ☐ This exercise is most difficult in the book.

READING AND SPEAKING
Three musical cities

1 **T 10.6** Listen to three types of music. What kind of music is it? Which music goes with which city?

New Orleans   **Vienna**   **Liverpool**

2 Where are these cities? What do you know about them? Each sentence is about one of them. Write **N**, **V**, or **L**.

1. _**V**_ Its music, theater, museums, and parks make it a popular tourist center.
2. ___ It stands on the banks of the Mississippi River.
3. ___ It stands on the banks of the River Danube.
4. ___ It is an important port for travel to Ireland.
5. ___ In 1762, King Louis XV of France gave it to his cousin Carlos of Spain.
6. ___ Its university, founded in 1365, is one of the oldest in Europe.
7. ___ It became an important trade center for sugar, spices, and slaves.
8. ___ It has a French Quarter with many old buildings and excellent cajun restaurants.

3 Work in three groups.

Group 1 Read about **New Orleans**.
Group 2 Read about **Vienna**.
Group 3 Read about **Liverpool**.

Which sentences in Exercise 2 are about your city?

4 Answer the questions about your city.

1. How many people live there?
2. What is the name of its river?
3. Why is it a tourist center?
4. What are some important dates in its history?
5. Which famous people lived there?
6. What kind of music is it famous for?
7. What else is world famous about the city?
8. Which of these things can you do in the city you read about?

- go by ship to Ireland
- see Sigmund Freud's house
- see a famous carnival
- listen to great jazz
- listen to a famous orchestra
- visit the homes of a famous rock group

5 Find partners from the other two groups. Compare the cities, using your answers.

Your hometown

6 Write some similar information about your city, town, or village. Tell a partner or the class.

New Orleans

New Orleans is the largest city in the state of Louisiana. It stands on the banks of the Mississippi River and is a busy port and tourist center. Its population of 550,000 is very cosmopolitan, with immigrants from many countries. Every year people from all over the world visit New Orleans to see its famous Mardi Gras carnival.

Its history

In 1682 the French named Louisiana after the French King, Louis XIV. They built New Orleans in 1718. In 1762, Louis XV gave it to his cousin Carlos of Spain. Then, in 1800, it became French again until Napoleon sold it to the United States in 1803. The French Quarter in New Orleans still has many old buildings and excellent cajun restaurants.

Its music

New Orleans is the home of jazz. Jazz is a mixture of blues, dance songs, and hymns. Black musicians started to play jazz in the late 19th century. Louis Armstrong and Jelly Roll Morton came from the city. New Orleans is most famous for its jazz, but it also has a philharmonic orchestra.

Vienna

Vienna, or *Wien* in German, is the capital of Austria. It stands on the banks of the River Danube and is the gateway between east and west Europe. Its music, theater, museums, and parks make it a popular tourist center. It has a population of over 1,500,000.

Its history

Vienna has a rich history. Its university opened in 1365, and is one of the oldest in Europe. From 1558 to 1806 it was the center of the Holy Roman Empire and it became an important cultural center of art and learning in the 18th and 19th centuries. The famous psychiatrist, Sigmund Freud, lived and worked here.

Its music

Vienna was the music capital of the world for many centuries. Haydn, Mozart, Beethoven, Brahms, Schubert, and the Strauss family all came to work here. It is now the home of one of the world's most famous orchestra's, the Vienna Philharmonic. Its State Opera House is also world famous.

Liverpool

Liverpool is Britain's second biggest port, after London. It stands on the banks of the River Mersey in northwest England. It is an important passenger port for travel to Ireland, and many Irish immigrants live there. It has a population of 448,300.

Its history

King John named Liverpool in 1207. The city grew bigger in the 18th century, when it became an important center for trading sugar, spices, and slaves between Africa, Britain, the Americas, and the West Indies.

Its music

Liverpool's most famous musicians are the Beatles. In the 1960s this British rock group was popular all over the world. They had 30 top ten hits. They were all born in Liverpool and started the group there in 1959. They first played at a nightclub called the Cavern and then traveled the world. One of them, Paul McCartney, is now the richest musician in the world. Many tourists visit Liverpool to see the homes of the Beatles.

VOCABULARY AND PRONUNCIATION
City and country words

City	Country	Both
park		

1 Find these words in the picture. Which things do you usually find in cities? Which in the country? Which in both? Put the words into the correct columns.

woods park museum church skyscraper farm bridge parking lot seaport factory field
theater nightclub lake hill mountain apartment building river bank tractor house

2 Complete the sentences with a word from Exercise 1.

1. Mount Everest is the highest _____ in the world.
2. The Golden Gate _____ in San Francisco is the longest _____ in the United States.
3. The Caspian Sea isn't a sea. It's the largest _____ in the world.
4. Singapore is the busiest _____ in Asia. Ships from all over the world stop there.
5. The Empire State Building in New York was the tallest _____ in the world for over 40 years.

3 Match the words to their pronunciation.

   a. /wʊdz/ _____   c. /fɑrm/ _____   e. /ˈtræktər/ _____
   b. /ˈfæktəri/ _____   d. /fild/ _____   f. /brɪdʒ/ _____

T 10.7 Listen and check your answers. Then listen and repeat.

4 Do you prefer the city or the country? Divide into two groups. Play the game. Which group can continue the longest?

Group 1 A walk in the country
Continue one after the other.
S1 I went for a walk in the country and I saw a farm.
S2 I went for a walk in the country and I saw a farm and some cows.
S3 I went for …

Group 2 A walk in the city
Continue one after the other.
S1 I went for a walk in the city and I saw some stores.
S2 I went for a walk in the city and I saw some stores and a nightclub.
S3 I went for …

EVERYDAY ENGLISH
Directions 2

1 **T 10.8** Listen to the directions to the lake. Mark the route on the map. Then fill in the blanks.

"Drive __along__ Park Road and turn _____ . Go _____ the bridge and _____ the church. Turn _____ up the hill then _____ _____ after the farm. Drive _____ the hill to the river. Then, go over the bridge. The lake is _____ _____ right. It takes 20 minutes."

2 **T 10.9** Complete the text with the prepositions. Listen to Norm talking about his drive in the country. Check your answers.

along	down	into	out of	over	past	through	under	up

NORM'S DRIVE IN THE COUNTRY

Norman drove

__out of__ the garage,

_____ the road, and

_____ the bridge.

Then he drove

_____ the church,

_____ the hill, and

_____ the hill.

Next he drove

_____ the river,

_____ the bushes,

and _____ the lake!

3 Cover the text. Look at the pictures and tell Norm's story.

4 Work with a partner.   **Student A** Think of a place near your school. Give your partner directions, but don't say what the place is!
   Student B Listen to the directions. Where are you?

11 Looking good!

Present Continuous · Whose? · Clothes · Words that rhyme · In a clothing store

STARTER

1 Look around the classroom. Can you see any of these clothes?

> a hat   a coat   a sweater   a shirt   a T-shirt   a dress   a skirt   a jacket
> a suit   pants   jeans   shorts   shoes   sneakers   boots

2 What are you wearing?
What is your teacher wearing?
Tell the class.

> *I'm wearing blue jeans and a white T-shirt.*

> *She's wearing a dress.*

DESCRIBING PEOPLE
Present Continuous

1 Look at the photographs. Describe the people.

Who . . . ?
• is tall   • isn't very tall   • is pretty good-looking   • is handsome

Who has . . . ?

| long
short
blonde
brown
gray | hair | blue
brown | eyes |

> *Donna has brown hair and brown eyes.*

2 What are they doing?

Who . . . ?
• is smiling   • is cooking
• is talking   • is standing up
• is writing   • is playing
• is laughing   • is running
• is eating   • is sitting down

> *Cathy's smiling.*   > *Angela's running.*

3 What are they wearing?

> *Jamal is wearing a brown T-shirt.*

Sue, Cathy, and Janet

Keiko

Jamal

Flora and Toni

Angela

Ryan

Oscar and Luis

Scott

Donna

PRACTICE

Who is it?

1 Work with a partner.

Student A Choose someone in the classroom, but
don't say who.

Student B Ask Yes/No questions to find out who it is!

Is it a girl?

Yes, it is.

Is she sitting near the window?

No, she isn't.

Does she have blonde hair?

No, she doesn't.

2 Write sentences that are true for you at the moment.

1. I/wearing a jacket
   I'm not wearing a jacket, I'm wearing a sweater.
2. I/wearing jeans
3. I/standing up
4. I/looking out of the window
5. It/raining
6. teacher/writing
7. We/working hard
8. I/chewing gum

Tell a partner about yourself.

Who's at the party?

3 **T 11.1** Alan is at Monica's party, but he doesn't know anyone. Monica is telling him about the other guests. Listen and write the names above the people.

4 Listen again and complete the table.

	Present Continuous	Present Simple
Harry	He's sitting down, and he's talking to Wendy.	He works in L.A.
Wendy		
Laura		
George		
Rita and Sam		

5 Work with a partner.

Student A Look at the picture of the party on page 119. *Don't* look at your partner's picture.

Student B Look at the picture of the party on page 120. *Don't* look at your partner's picture.

A DAY IN THE PARK
Whose is it?

1 Find these things in the picture.

> a baseball cap   a bicycle   a soccer ball
> inline skates   sneakers   a dog   sunglasses   a radio
> a skateboard   an umbrella   flowers

2 **T 11.2** Listen to the questions. Complete the answers with *his*, *hers*, or *theirs*.

1. Whose baseball cap is this?   It's _____ .
2. Whose flowers are these?   They're _____ .
3. Whose dog is this?   It's _____ .

Point to the other things in the picture. Ask and answer questions about them.

3 Give something of yours to the teacher. Ask and answer questions about the objects. Use these possessive pronouns.

> mine   yours   his   hers   ours   theirs

Whose jacket is this?   *It's Ella's.*   *It's hers.*

Is it yours, Ella?   *Yes, it's mine.*

PRACTICE

who's or whose?

1 Choose the correct word. Compare your answers with a partner.
1. I like *your* / *yours* house.
2. *Ours* / *Our* house is smaller than *their* / *theirs*.
3. And *their* / *theirs* yard is bigger than *our* / *ours*, too.
4. *My* / *Mine* children are older than *her* / *hers*.
5. *Whose* / *Who's* talking to *your* / *yours* sister?
6. This book isn't *my* / *mine*. Is it *your* / *yours*?
7. "*Whose* / *Who's* dictionary is this?" "It's *his* / *him*."
8. "*Whose* / *Who's* going to the party tonight?" "I'm not."
9. "*Whose* / *Who's* dog is running around in *our* / *ours* yard?" "It's John's."

2 **T 11.3** Listen to the sentences.

If the word is *Whose?* shout **1**! If the word is *Who's?* shout **2**!

What a mess!

3 **T 11.4** The house is a mess!
Complete the conversation.
Listen and check.

A _____ tennis racket _____ this?

B It's _____ .

A What's it doing here?

B I'm _____ tennis this afternoon.

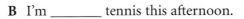

> ❗ The Present Continuous can also describe activities happening in the near future.
> I**'m playing** tennis this afternoon.
> We**'re having** pizza for dinner tonight.

4 Make more conversations with a partner.
1. sunglasses … these? / John's / going to the beach later
2. shoes … these? / Mary's / going dancing tonight
3. suitcase … this? / mine / going on vacation tomorrow
4. coat … this? / Jane's / leaving soon
5. plane ticket … this? / Amy's / flying to Miami this afternoon
6. glasses … these? / ours / having a party tonight

Check it

5 Correct the sentences.
1. Who's boots are these?
2. I'm wearing a jeans.
3. There's Roger. He stands next to Jeremy.
4. He's work in a bank. He's the manager.
5. What is drinking Suzie?
6. Whose that man in the front yard?
7. Where you going tonight?

GRAMMAR SPOT

1 Complete the table.

Subject	Object	Adjective	Pronoun
I	me	my	mine
you	you	_____	_____
he	_____	his	_____
she	_____	_____	hers
we	us	our	_____
they	them	_____	_____

2 *Whose . . . ?* asks about possession.
Whose hat is this?
Whose shoes are these?   It's mine. = It's my hat.
Whose is it?

3 Careful!
Who's your teacher?   Who's = Who is

▶▶ **Grammar Reference 11.3 p. 142**

LISTENING AND SPEAKING
What a wonderful world!

1 Look out of the window. What can you see?
Buildings? Hills? Fields? Can you see any people?
What are they doing? Describe the scene.

2 These words often go together. Match them.
Can you see any of them in the photographs?

shake	clouds
babies	roses
sunny	hands
starry	trees
blue	day
red	night
white	cry
green	bloom
flowers	of the rainbow
colors	skies

3 Read this song by Louis Armstrong.
Can you complete any of the lines?
Many of the words are from Exercise 2.

4 **T 11.5** Listen and complete the song.

What do you think?

Make a list of things that *you* think are
wonderful in the world. Compare your
list with a partner.

What a Wonderful World

I see ___trees___ of green

red _____ too

I see them _____ for me and you

and I think to myself

what a wonderful world.

I see _____ of blue

and _____ of white

the bright _____ day

the dark _____ night

and I think to myself

what a wonderful world.

The _____ of the rainbow

so pretty in the sky

are also on the _____

of the people going by.

I see friends shaking _____

saying, "How do you do?"

They're really saying

"I _____ you."

I hear _____ cry

I watch them grow.

They'll _____ much more

than you'll ever know

and I think to myself

what a wonderful world.

Yes, I think to myself

what a wonderful world.

VOCABULARY AND PRONUNCIATION
Words that rhyme

1 Match the words that rhyme.

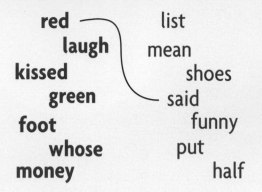

red — list
laugh   mean
kissed   shoes
green   said
foot   funny
whose   put
money   half

white   brown
town   night
they   knows
rose   noise
boys   pay

2 Write another word that has the same sound.

Vowels

1. /ɛ/ _red_ _said_   5. /ʊ/ _foot_ _____
2. /æ/ _laugh_ _____   6. /u/ _shoes_ _____
3. /ɪ/ _list_ _____   7. /ʌ/ _funny_ _____
4. /i/ _mean_ _____

Diphthongs

1. /aɪ/ _white_ _____   4. /oʊ/ _rose_ _____
2. /aʊ/ _brown_ _____   5. /ɔɪ/ _noise_ _____
3. /eɪ/ _pay_ _____

T 11.6 Listen and check.

3 Can you add any more words to the lists?

Tongue twisters

4 **T 11.7** Tongue twisters are sentences that are difficult to say. They are good pronunciation practice. Listen, then try saying these quickly to a partner.

1. Four fine fresh fish for you

2. Six silly sisters selling shiny shoes

3. If a dog chews shoes, whose shoes does he choose?

4. I'm looking back,
To see if she's looking back,
To see if I'm looking back,
To see if she's looking back
at me!

5 Choose two tongue twisters and learn them. Say them to the class.

EVERYDAY ENGLISH
In a clothing store

1 Read the lines of conversation. Who says them, the customer or the salesperson? Write **C** or **SP**.

a. <u>SP</u> Can I help you?

b. <u>C</u> Yes, I like that one much better. Can I try it on?

c. ___ $34.99. How do you want to pay?

d. ___ Yes, I'm looking for a shirt to go with my new suit.

e. ___ Blue.

f. ___ Yes, of course. The fitting rooms are over there.

g. ___ OK. I'll take the white. How much is it?

h. ___ Can I pay by credit card?

i. ___ What color are you looking for?

j. ___ No, it's not the right blue.

k. ___ No, it's too big. Do you have a smaller size?

l. ___ I'm sorry, that's the last blue one we have. But we have a smaller size in white.

m. ___ Well, what about this one? It's a darker blue.

n. ___ How about this one? Do you like it?

o. ___ Is the size OK?

p. ___ Credit card's fine. Thank you very much.

2 Can you match any lines?

Can I help you?

Yes, I'm looking for a shirt to go with my new suit.

How about this one? Do you like it?

No, it's not the right blue.

3 Work with a partner and put the all the lines in the correct order.

T 11.8 Listen and check.

4 Practice the conversation with your partner. Make more conversations in a clothing store. Buy some different clothes.

12 Life's an adventure!

going to future · Infinitive of purpose · The weather · Making suggestions

1 How many sentences can you make?

| I'm going to Florida
I went to Florida | soon.
when I was a student.
next month.
next year.
two years ago.
when I retire. |

2 Make similar true sentences about you. Tell the class.

FUTURE PLANS
going to

1 Nadia and her teacher, Ms. Bishop, both have plans for the future. Read their future plans. Which do you think are Nadia's? Which are Ms. Bishop's? Write **N** or **MB**.

1. ___ I'm going to be a ballet dancer.
2. ___ I'm going to travel all over the world.
3. ___ I'm going to learn Russian.
4. ___ I'm going to learn to drive.
5. ___ I'm going to open a school.
6. ___ I'm not going to get married until I'm thirty-five.
7. ___ I'm not going to wear skirts and blouses.
8. ___ I'm going to wear jeans and T-shirts all the time.
9. ___ I'm going to write a book.
10. ___ I'm going to become a TV star.

T 12.1 Listen and check. Were you correct?

2 Talk first about Nadia, then about Ms. Bishop. Use the ideas in Exercise 1.

> *Nadia's going to be a ballet dancer.*

> *She's going to …*   > *She isn't going to …*

Which two plans are the same for both of them?

> *They're both going to …*

When I grow up …

Nadia, age 11

3 **T 12.2** Listen and repeat the questions and answers about Nadia.

> Is she going to be a ballet dancer?

> Yes, she is.

> What's she going to do?

> Travel all over the world.

GRAMMAR SPOT

1 The verb *to be* + *going to* expresses future plans. Complete the table.

I	_____	
You	_____	
He/She	_____	going to leave tomorrow.
We	_____	
They	_____	

What are the questions and the negatives?

2 Is there much difference between these two sentences?

I'm leaving tomorrow.   I'm going to leave tomorrow.

▶▶ **Grammar Reference 12.1 p. 143**

> When I retire ...

Ms. Bishop, age 59

PRACTICE

Questions about Nadia

1 With a partner, make more questions about Nadia. Then match them with an answer.

Questions

1. Why/she/learn French and Russian?
   Why is she going to learn French and Russian?
2. When/marry?
3. How many children/have?
4. How long/work?
5. What/teach?

Answers

____ a. Until she's seventy-five.
____ b. Two.
____ c. Dancing.
____ d. Not until she's thirty-five.
____ e. Because she wants to dance in Paris and Moscow.

2 **T 12.3** Listen and check. Practice the questions and answers with your partner.

Questions about you

3 Are you going to do any of these things after class today? Ask and answer the questions with a partner.

1. watch TV

> Are you going to watch TV?

> Yes, I am./No, I'm not.

2. have a cup of coffee
3. catch a bus
4. eat in a restaurant
5. meet some friends
6. cook a meal
7. go shopping
8. wash your hair
9. do your homework

4 Tell the class some of the things you and your partner *are* or *are not* going to do.

> We're both going to have some coffee.

> I'm going to catch a bus, but Anna isn't. She's going to walk home.

I'm going to sneeze!

> ❗ We also use *going to* when we can see *now* that something is sure to happen in the future.

5 What is going to happen? Use these verbs.

| have a baby   sneeze   win   jump   be late   kiss   rain   fall |

1. It **'s going to rain.**
2. You _____
3. I _____
4. They _____
5. She _____
6. He _____
7. He _____
8. They _____

6 Put a sentence from Exercise 5 into each blank.

1. Take an umbrella. **It's going to rain** .
2. Look! Jack's on the wall! _____ .
3. Anna's running very fast. _____ .
4. Look at the time! _____ for the meeting.
5. Look at that man! _____ .
6. _____ . It's due next month.
7. There's my sister and her boyfriend! Yuck! _____ .
8. "Oh, dear. _____ . *Aaaa-chooo!*" "Bless you!"

T 12.4 Listen and check.

I WANT TO TRAVEL THE WORLD
Infinitive of purpose

1 Match a country or a city with an activity. What can you see in the photographs?

London	travel down the Amazon
Paris	visit the Pyramids
Moscow	see Mount Fuji
Egypt	see the Eiffel Tower
Kenya	walk along the Great Wall
India	visit Ayer's Rock
China	take photographs of the lions
Japan	walk in Red Square
Australia	ride on a double-decker bus
Brazil	visit the Taj Mahal

2 Ms. Bishop is going to visit all these countries. She is telling her friend Harold about her plans. Read their conversation and complete the last sentence.

Ms. Bishop First I'm going to London.
Harold Why?
Ms. Bishop To ride on a double-decker bus, of course!
Harold Oh, yes! How wonderful! Where are you going after that?
Ms. Bishop Well, then I'm going to Paris to …

T 12.5 Listen and check.

GRAMMAR SPOT

1 With the verbs *to go* and *to come*, we usually use the Present Continuous for future plans.
   I'm going to France tomorrow.
   ✗ ~~I'm going to go~~ to France tomorrow.
   She's coming this evening.
   ✗ She's ~~going to come~~ this evening.

2 Do these sentences mean the same thing?
   I'm going to France to see the Eiffel Tower.
   I'm going to France because I want to see the Eiffel Tower.
   The infinitive can tell us why something happens.
   I'm going to the United States to learn English.

▶▶ **Grammar Reference 12.2 p. 143**

PRACTICE

Role play

1 Work with a partner. **Student A** is Harold, **Student B** is Ms. Bishop. Ask and answer questions about the places.

Harold   Why are you going to London?
Ms. Bishop To ride on a double-decker bus, of course!
Harold   How wonderful!

2 Talk about Ms. Bishop's trip. Use *first, then, next, after that.*

> *First she's going to London to ride on a double-decker bus. Then she's …*

Why and *When*?

3 Write down the names of some places you went to in the past. Ask and answer questions about the places with a partner.

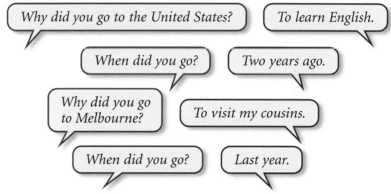

> *Why did you go to the United States?*
>
> *To learn English.*
>
> *When did you go?*
>
> *Two years ago.*
>
> *Why did you go to Melbourne?*
>
> *To visit my cousins.*
>
> *When did you go?*
>
> *Last year.*

Tell the class about your partner.

4 Write down the names of some places you are going to in the *future* and do the same.

> *Why are you going to Florida?*
>
> *To go to Disney World.*
>
> *When are you going?*
>
> *In two weeks.*

Check it

5 Put a check (✓) next to the correct sentence.

1. ☐ Is going to rain.
    ☐ It's going to rain.
2. ☐ Do you wash your hair this evening?
    ☐ Are you going to wash your hair this evening?
3. ☐ She's going to have a baby.
    ☐ She's going to has a baby.
4. ☐ I'm going to the post office to buy some stamps.
    ☐ I'm going to the post office for buy some stamps.
5. ☐ I'm going home early this evening.
    ☐ I'm go home early this evening.

READING AND SPEAKING
Living dangerously

1 Match a verb with a noun or phrase.

have	your job
win	an accident
quit	a class
take	good grades
get	a race

2 Which of these sports do you think is the *most* dangerous? Put them in order 1–6 (1 is the *most* dangerous). Compare your ideas with a partner and then the class.

- ☐ skiing
- ☐ soccer
- ☐ car racing
- ☐ windsurfing
- ☐ golf
- ☐ skydiving

3 Look at the photos of Jen Franchek and Mitch Cleveland. Which of their sports would you most like to try? Why?

Work in two groups.

Group A Read about Jen. **Group B** Read about Mitch.

Answer the questions about your person. Check your answers with your group.

1. What did he/she want to be as a child?
2. What job did he/she do when he/she grew up?
3. How did he/she become interested in the sport?
4. Why does he/she like the sport?
5. Does he/she think it is a dangerous sport?
6. Does he/she teach the sport?
7. What are his/her future plans?
8. When is she going to stop doing it?
9. These numbers are in your text. What do they refer to?
   3 8 30

4 Work with a partner from the other group. Compare Jen and Mitch, using your answers.

Interviews

1 **Group A** You are Jen. Make questions to ask Mitch.

1. Where/you grow up?
2. Why/do well at racing school?
3. Why/stop racing?
4. What/do next year?

Group B You are Mitch. Make questions to ask Jen.

1. When/do your first parachute jump?
2. Why/move to the country?
3. Why/love skydiving?
4. What/do next summer?

2 Work with a partner from the other group. Interview each other.

Jen Franchek

SKY DIVER

Jen Franchek was always interested in sports. When she was eight, she wanted to play baseball for the Atlanta Braves and be a jet pilot. But when she grew up, she didn't become a baseball player or a pilot, she became a computer programmer. When she was 23, she did a parachute jump with some friends and loved it. She decided that jumping out of airplanes was much more interesting than being a computer programmer, so she quit her job and moved to the country to learn parachute jumping and skydiving. She is now a full-time teacher of skydiving. She says:

"I love skydiving because it's so beautiful up there—blue sky, green fields, white clouds. The views are fantastic. You can see forever. It's so peaceful, you can forget about everything and relax. People think skydiving is dangerous, but it's very safe. Driving to the airport is much more dangerous. People have car accidents all the time, but when did you last hear of a skydiving accident? Next summer I'm going to do a skydive with 30 other women from 3 planes. That's a record. I'm never going to retire. I'm going to jump out of planes until I'm a little old lady!"

Mitch Cleveland

RACE-CAR DRIVER

Mitch Cleveland grew up in Brooklyn, Michigan, near the Michigan International Speedway and was always interested in cars. When he was eight years old, his grandfather took him to see his first race. That's when Mitch decided that he wanted to be a race-car driver. When he got older, Mitch became a test driver for General Motors and drove their new cars around the test track. Three years ago, when he was thirty, Mitch took a class at a racing school in California. He got the best grades in his class. So Mitch quit his job at GM and decided to become a professional racer. He says:

"I think I did well because I listened to everything the teacher said. I think my job as a test driver also helped. The best moment was my first professional race. I didn't win, but I came in fourth. Racing is great. I love the excitement. There's just nothing like it. It's a dangerous sport, but I like the danger. It's also very expensive. In fact, I stopped racing a year ago because it cost too much. I don't think I'm going to race again, I'm going to teach other people to drive. I'm going to open a driving school next year."

VOCABULARY AND SPEAKING
The weather

1 Match the words and symbols.

| sunny   rainy   windy   snowy   cloudy   foggy |

Which symbols can the following adjectives go with?

hot   warm   cold   cool   wet   dry

2 **T 12.6** Listen and complete the answers.

"What's the weather like today?" "It's _____ and _____."
"What was it like yesterday?" "Oh, it was _____ and _____."
"What's it going to be like tomorrow?" "I think it's going to be _____."

> The question *What . . . like?* asks for a description.
> What's the weather like? = Tell me about the weather.

Practice the questions and answers. Ask and answer about the weather where *you* are.

World weather

3 Work with a partner. Find out about the weather around the world.
Student A Look at the information on this page.
Student B Look at the information on page 121.

Ask and answer questions to complete the information.

> *What was the weather like in Atlanta?*

> *It was sunny and hot. Thirty degrees.*

WORLD WEATHER: NOON YESTERDAY

		°C
Atlanta	*S*	*30*
Boston	—	—
Brasilia	S	24
Denver	—	—
Hong Kong	R	16
London	—	—
Los Angeles	Fg	21
Mexico City	—	—
San Francisco	Fg	10
São Paulo	—	—
Seattle	R	6
Toronto	—	—
Vancouver	Sn	4

S = sunny
C = cloudy
Fg = foggy
R = rainy
Sn = snowy

4 Which city was the hottest? Which was the coldest?
Which month do you think it is?

EVERYDAY ENGLISH
Making suggestions

1 Make a list of things you can do in good weather and things you can do in bad weather. Compare your list with a partner.

Good Weather	Bad Weather
Go to the beach	Watch TV

2 **T 12.7** Read and listen to the beginning of two conversations. Complete B's suggestions.

1. **A** It's a beautiful day!
    What should we do?
    B Let's _____ !

2. **A** It's raining again!
    What should we do?
    B Let's _____ and _____ .

> **!** **1** We use *should* to ask for and make suggestions.
> What should we do? = What do you want to do?
> Should we go swimming? = I suggest that we go swimming.
> **2** We use *Let's* to make a suggestion for everyone.
> Let's go! = I suggest that we all go. (Let's = Let us)
> Let's have a pizza!

3 Match these lines with the two conversations in Exercise 2. Put them in the correct order to complete the conversations.

Well, let's go to the beach.	But we just watched a video last night.
OK. What movie do you want to see?	OK. I'll get my bathing suit.
Oh, no! It's too hot to play tennis.	Well, let's go to the movies.

T 12.8 Listen and check. Practice the conversations with your partner.

4 Have more conversations suggesting what to do when the weather is good or bad. Use your lists of activities in Exercise 1 to help you.

13 You're pretty smart!

STARTER

1 Match a question word with an answer.

2 Look at the answers. What do you think the story is?

When . . . ?	Six.
Where . . . ?	1991.
What . . . ?	Paris.
Who . . . ?	Because I love him.
Why . . . ?	John.
Which . . . ?	Some roses.
How . . . ?	$50.
How much . . . ?	The red ones.
How many . . . ?	By plane.

A QUIZ
Question words

1 Work in groups and answer the quiz.

2 **T 13.1** Listen and check your answers. Listen carefully to the intonation of the questions.

GRAMMAR SPOT

1 Underline all the question words in the quiz.

2 Make *two* questions for each of these statements, one with a question word and one without.

I live in Florida. (where)

"Where do you live?" "Florida."
"Do you live in Florida?" "Yes, I do."

1. She's wearing jeans. (what)
2. She works at the bank. (where)
3. He's leaving tomorrow. (when)
4. I visited my aunt. (who)
5. We came by taxi. (how)
6. They're going to have a party. (why)

3 What are the short answers to the questions?

▶▶ **Grammar Reference 13.1 p. 143**

3 In groups, write some general knowledge questions. Ask the class!

 **GENERAL KN**

1 When did the first person walk on the moon?
a. 1961 b. 1965 c. 1969

2 Where are the Alps?

3 Who lives at 1600 Pennsylvania Avenue in Washington, D.C.?

4 Who won the 1994 World Cup?

5 How many states are there in the United States?

6 How much does an African elephant weigh?
a. 3–5 tons b. 5–7 tons c. 7–9 tons

7 How far is it from Tokyo, Japan, to New York City?
a. 5,000 km b. 10,000 km c. 15,000 km

8 How old was Princess Diana when she died?
a. 33 b. 36 c. 39

PRACTICE

Questions and answers

1 Look at the question words in **A** and the answers in **C**. Choose the correct question from **B**.

> *Where did you go?*   *To the mall.*

A	B	C
Where		To the mall.
What		A new jacket.
When	did you buy?	This morning.
Who	did you go?	A friend from work.
Why	did you go with?	To buy some new clothes.
Which one	did you pay?	The black leather one.
How		We drove.
How much		$189.99.
How many		Only one.

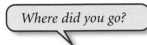

OWLEDGE QUIZ

9 What languages do Canadians speak?

10 What did Marconi invent in 1901?
a. the radio   b. the television   c. the computer

11 What kind of music did Louis Armstrong play?
a. jazz   b. classical   c. rock

12 What happens at the end of *Romeo and Juliet*?

13 What happened to Nelson Mandela in 1994?

14 Why do birds migrate?

15 Which was the first country to have TV?
a. Britain   b. the United States   c. Russia

16 Which language has the most words?
a. French   b. Chinese   c. English

Listening and pronunciation

2 **T 13.2** Put a check (✓) next to the sentence you hear.

1. ☐ Where do you want to go?
   ☐ Why do you want to go?

2. ☐ How is she?
   ☐ Who is she?

3. ☐ Where's he staying?
   ☐ Where's she staying?

4. ☐ Why did they come?
   ☐ Why didn't they come?

5. ☐ How old was she?
   ☐ How old is she?

6. ☐ Does he play the guitar?
   ☐ Did he play the guitar?

7. ☐ Where did you go to school?
   ☐ Where do you go to school?

Asking about you

3 Put the words in the correct order to make questions.

1. like learning do English you?
   Do you like learning English?

2. do you night what did last?
   _____

3. languages mother many does how your speak?
   _____

4. last go you shopping did when?
   _____

5. sport which you do like best?
   _____

6. come car today school by you to did?
   _____

7. many do own CDs you how?
   _____

8. usually who sit you do next class in to?
   _____

9. English want learn to you do why?
   _____

4 Work with a partner. Ask and answer the questions.

DO IT CAREFULLY!
Adverbs and adjectives

1 Are the words in *italics* adjectives or adverbs?

1. Smoking is a *bad* habit. **adjective**
   The team played *badly* and lost the game.
2. Please listen *carefully*.
   Jane's a *careful* driver.
3. The homework was *easy*.
   Peter's very good at tennis. He won the game *easily*.
4. I know the prime minister *well*.
   My husband's a *good* cook.
5. It's a *hard* life.
   Teachers work *hard* and don't earn much money.

> ### GRAMMAR SPOT
>
> **1** Look at these sentences.
>   Lunch is a quick meal for many people.
>   (*quick* = adjective. It describes a noun.)
>   I ate my lunch quickly.
>   (*quickly* = adverb. It describes a verb.)
>
> **2** How do we make regular adverbs? What happens when the adjective ends in *-y*?
>
> **3** There are two irregular adverbs in Exercise 1. Find them.
>
> ▶▶ **Grammar Reference 13.2 p. 143**

2 Match the verbs or phrases with an adverb. Usually more than one answer is possible. Which are the irregular adverbs?

get up	slowly
walk	quietly
work	early
run	fluently
speak	carefully
speak English	easily
pass the test	hard
do your homework	fast/quickly

PRACTICE

Order of adjectives/adverbs

1 Put the adjective in parentheses in the correct place in the sentence. Where necessary, change the adjective to an adverb.

1. We went to England, but unfortunately we had weather. (terrible)
   We went to England, but unfortunately we had terrible weather.
2. Maria dances. (good)
3. When I saw the accident, I called the police. (immediate)
4. Don't worry. Justin is a driver. (careful)
5. My son is a teenager. He loves cars, music, and girls. (typical)
6. Please speak. I can't understand you. (slow)
7. We had a test today. (easy)
8. We all passed. (easy)
9. You speak English. (good)

Telling a story

2 Complete these sentences in a suitable way.

1. It started to rain. **Fortunately** …
2. Peter invited me to his party. **Unfortunately** …
3. I was fast asleep when **suddenly** …
4. I saw a man with a gun outside the bank. **Immediately** …

3 [T 13.3] Look at the picture and listen to a man describing what happened to him in the middle of the night. Number the adverbs in the order you hear them.

____ quickly
____ quietly
____ slowly
____ immediately
____ carefully
_1_ suddenly
____ fortunately
____ really

Noises in the night

4 Work with a partner and tell the story again. Use the order of the adverbs to help you.

Check it

5 Each sentence has a mistake. Find it and correct it.

1. Where does live Anna's sister?   **Where does Anna's sister live?**
2. The children came into the classroom noisyly.
3. What means *whistle*?
4. I always work hardly.
5. Do you can help me, please?
6. When is going Peter on vacation?

VOCABULARY
Describing feelings

1 Match the feelings to the pictures.

bored   tired   worried   excited   annoyed   interested

2 Match the feelings and reasons to make sentences.

	Feelings		Reasons
I am	bored tired worried excited annoyed interested	because	I'm going on vacation tomorrow. we have a good teacher. I worked very hard today. I can't find my keys. I don't have anything to do. I want to go to the party but I can't.

> **!** Some adjectives can end in both *-ed* and *-ing*.
> I was <u>interested</u> in the book.
> The book was <u>interesting</u>.
> The students were <u>bored</u>.
> The lesson was <u>boring</u>.

3 Complete each sentence with the correct adjective.

1. **excited, exciting**
   Life in New York is very …
   The soccer fans were very …
2. **tired, tiring**
   The marathon runners were very …
   That game of tennis was very …
3. **annoyed, annoying**
   The loud music was really …
   The teacher was … when nobody did the homework.
4. **worried, worrying**
   This news is very …
   Everybody was very … when they heard the news.

4 Answer these questions using adjectives from Exercises 1 and 2.

- How do you feel before a test?
- How do you feel after a test?
- Do you like soccer? Why/Why not?
- How do you feel if your friend is late?
- Did you enjoy the last movie you saw? Why/Why not?

READING AND LISTENING
A story in a story

1 Think about when you were a small child. Did your parents tell you stories? Which was your favorite story? Tell the class.

2 Look at the first picture. Who do you think the people on the train are? Do they know each other?

3 **T 13.4** Read and listen to Part One of the story.

4 Answer the questions.
1. Who are the people on the train?
2. What does Cyril ask questions about?
3. Why does the aunt tell the children a story?
4. What is the story about?
5. Do the children like the story?
6. Why does the young man start speaking?
7. Which of these adjectives best describe the people? Write them in the correct column.

> quiet   noisy   badly behaved   tired
> worried   bored   boring   annoyed
> annoying

The aunt
tired

The children

The young man

A TRAIN JOURNEY

The people on the train were hot and tired. A tall young man sat next to three small children and their aunt. The aunt and the children talked. When the aunt spoke she always began with "Don't …" When the children spoke they always began with "Why … ?" The young man said nothing.

The small boy whistled loudly. "Don't do that, Cyril," said his aunt. Cyril stood up and looked out of the window at the countryside.
"Why is that man taking those sheep out of that field?" he asked.
"Perhaps he's taking them to another field where there's more grass," said the aunt.
"But there's lots of grass in that field. Why can't the sheep stay there?"

73

"Perhaps the grass in the other field is better."

"Why is it better?"

The young man looked annoyed.

"Oh, dear," thought the aunt, "he doesn't like children."

"Sit down quietly, Cyril. Now, listen, I'm going to tell you all a story."

The children looked bored but they listened. The story was very boring indeed. It was about a very beautiful little girl, who worked hard and behaved beautifully. Everybody loved her. One day she fell into a lake and everyone in the village ran to save her.

"Why did they save her?" asked the bigger girl.

"Because she was so good," said the aunt.

"But that's stupid," said the girl. "When people fall into lakes, it doesn't matter if they're good or bad, you run to save them."

"You're right," said the young man, speaking for the first time. "That's a ridiculous story."

"Well, perhaps you would like to tell a story," said the aunt coldly.

"OK," said the man. The children looked interested and he began.

6 **T 13.5** Read and listen to Part Two.

74

The tale of horribly good Bertha

"Once upon a time, a long time ago there was a little girl called Bertha. She was always well-behaved and worked hard at school to please her parents and her teachers. She was never late, never dirty, never rude, and she never told lies."

The children on the train began to look bored. "Was she pretty?" asked the smaller girl.
"No," said the young man. "She wasn't pretty at all. She was just horribly good. Bertha was so good that she won three gold medals. One said *Never Late*, one said *Always Polite*, and the third said *Best Child in the World*."

"Yuck!" said the three children.

"Anyway," said the young man, "Bertha was so good that the king invited her to his palace. So she put on her best clean white dress and she pinned her three medals to the

75

front, and she walked through the woods to the king's palace. But in the woods there lived a big hungry wolf. He saw Bertha's lovely white dress through the trees and he heard the medals clinking together as she walked.

"'Aha!' thought the wolf. 'Lunch!' And he started to move quickly but quietly through the trees toward Bertha.'"

"Oh, no!" cried the children. "Is he going to eat Bertha?"

"Yes, of course," answered the young man. "Bertha tried to run away, but she couldn't run fast because the medals were so heavy. The wolf caught her easily and he ate everything, every bit of Bertha, except her three medals."

"That's a terrible story," said the aunt.
"No, it isn't," shouted the children. "It's the best story ever!"
"Ah," said the young man, "the train's stopping. It's my station."

7 Answer the questions.

1. What is the same and what is different in the aunt's story and the young man's story?
2. Does the aunt like the young man's story? Why/Why not?
3. Do the children like the story? Why/Why not?
4. Which of these do you think is the moral of Bertha's story?

> It pays to be good.
> It never pays to be good.
> It doesn't always pay to be good.

8 Tell the story of Bertha. Use the pictures in Exercise 5 on page 99 to help you.

Language work

1 Put some adjectives and adverbs from the story of Bertha into the correct box.

Adjectives	Adverbs
hot	loudly

2 Write questions about Bertha's story using these question words. Ask and answer the questions across the class.

> ~~when~~ how many what why where what how

> *When did the story take place?*

> *A long time ago.*

EVERYDAY ENGLISH

Catching a train

1 Ann is calling to find out the times of trains to New York.

 T 13.6 Listen and complete the timetable.

2 **T 13.7** Ann is at South Station in Boston. Listen and complete the conversation. Then practice with a partner.

A Good morning. (1) _Can you tell me_ the times of the trains (2) _____ New York (3) _____ to South Station, please?

B When (4) _____ come back? Afternoon? Evening?

A About five o'clock this afternoon.

B About (5) _____ Let's see … Well, there's a train that (6) _____ New York at 4:30 … then there isn't (7) _____ until 6:45.

A And (8) _____ get in?

B The 4:30 train gets in to South Station at 9:15 and the 6:45 (9) _____

A OK. Thanks a lot.

3 Ann goes to the ticket office. Put the lines of the conversation in the correct order.

___ **A** Hello. A round-trip ticket to New York, please.
___ **C** That's eighty-five dollars.
___ **A** Thank you. Which platform is it?
___ **C** Platform 1. Over there.
___ **A** Here's a hundred.
___ **C** How do you want to pay?
_9_ **A** Thank you.
___ **C** Here's your change and your ticket.
___ **A** Cash, please.

 T 13.8 Listen and check. Practice the conversation with a partner.

Getting information

4 Make more conversations with your partner. Look at the timetable on page 122. Decide where you want to go. Find out about times, then buy your ticket.

DEPARTURE TIME BOSTON	ARRIVAL TIME NEW YORK
7:55	
10:30	
12:30	

14 Have you ever?

Present Perfect + *ever*, *never*, and *yet* · At the airport

1 Match the countries and flags.

Australia	Brazil	Mexico	Thailand	Korea	the United Kingdom
Argentina	France	Japan	Canada	Spain	the United States

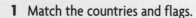

1. **Thailand** 2. _____ 3. _____ 4. _____ 5. _____ 6. _____

7. _____ 8. _____ 9. _____ 10. _____ 11. _____ 12. _____

2 Put a check (✓) next to the countries that you have visited.

IN MY LIFE
Present Perfect + *ever* and *never*

1 **T 14.1** Read and listen to the sentences. Then listen and repeat.

I've been to Korea. (I've = I have)
I haven't been to Japan.
I've been to Canada.
I've never been to Australia.
I haven't been to any of these countries!

Work in groups. Tell each other which of the countries above you have or haven't been to. Have you been to any other countries?

2 **T 14.2** Read and listen to the conversation. Practice with a partner.

A Have you ever been to Tokyo?
B No, I haven't.
A Have you ever been to Seoul?
B Yes, I have.
A When did you go?
B Two years ago.

3 Write down the names of four cities in your country or another country that you have been to. Have similar conversations with your partner.

4 Tell the class about your partner.

> Min's been to Seoul.   (Min's = Min has)

> She went there two years ago.

> But she hasn't been to Tokyo. / She's never been to Tokyo.   (She's = She has)

GRAMMAR SPOT

1 We use the Present Perfect to talk about experiences in our lives.
   Have you ever (at any time in your life) been to Toronto?

2 We use the Past Simple to say exactly *when* something happened.
   When did you go to Toronto?

I went there	last year.
	two years ago.
	in 1998.

3 We make the Present Perfect tense with *has/have* + the past participle.
   Complete the table.

	Affirmative	Negative	
I/you/we/they	_____	_____	been to Paris.
He/she/it	_____	_____	

4 Write *ever* and *never* in the right place in these sentences.
   Has he _____ been to Hong Kong?
   He's _____ been to Hong Kong.

▶▶ **Grammar Reference 14.1 p. 144**

PRACTICE

Past participles

1 Here are the past participles of some verbs. Write the infinitive.

eaten	**eat**	made	_____	given	_____
seen	_____	taken	_____	won	_____
met	_____	driven	_____	had	_____
drunk	_____	cooked	_____	stayed	_____
flown	_____	bought	_____	done	_____

2 Which are the two regular verbs?

3 What is the Past Simple form of all the verbs?

4 Look at the list of irregular verbs on page 152 and check your answers.

The life of Ryan

1 **T 14.3** Listen to Ryan talking about his life and put a check (✓) next to the things he has done.

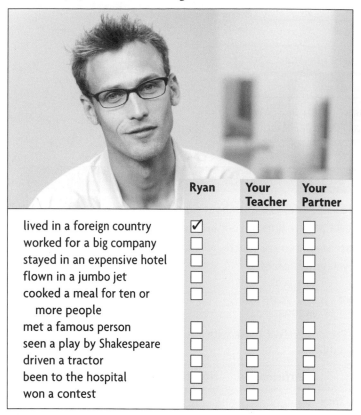

	Ryan	Your Teacher	Your Partner
lived in a foreign country	✓	☐	☐
worked for a big company	☐	☐	☐
stayed in an expensive hotel	☐	☐	☐
flown in a jumbo jet	☐	☐	☐
cooked a meal for ten or more people	☐	☐	☐
met a famous person	☐	☐	☐
seen a play by Shakespeare	☐	☐	☐
driven a tractor	☐	☐	☐
been to the hospital	☐	☐	☐
won a contest	☐	☐	☐

2 Tell your teacher about Ryan and answer your teacher's questions.

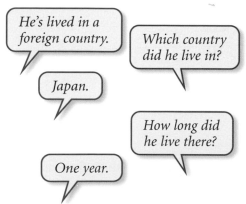

He's lived in a foreign country.

Which country did he live in?

Japan.

How long did he live there?

One year.

3 Ask your teacher the questions and complete the chart.

Have you ever lived in a foreign country?

Which country did you live in?

4 Ask a partner the questions. Tell the class about your partner.

A HONEYMOON IN NEW YORK
Present Perfect + *yet*

1 Rod and Marilyn come from Edmonton, Alberta, Canada. They are on their honeymoon in New York. Before they went, they made a list of things they wanted to do there. Read the list below.

2 **T 14.4** Marilyn is calling her sister Judy, back home in Canada. Listen to their conversation. Put a check (✓) next to the things she and Rod have done.

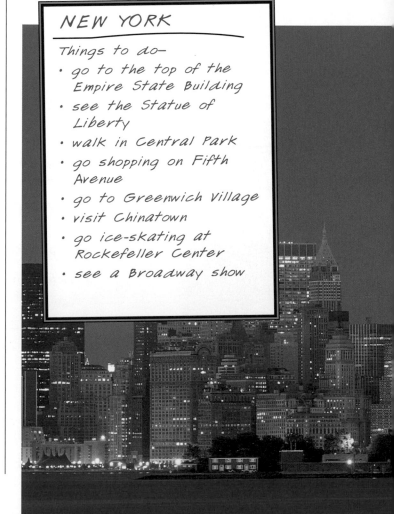

NEW YORK

Things to do–
• go to the top of the Empire State Building
• see the Statue of Liberty
• walk in Central Park
• go shopping on Fifth Avenue
• go to Greenwich Village
• visit Chinatown
• go ice-skating at Rockefeller Center
• see a Broadway show

GRAMMAR SPOT

1 Complete the sentences.
  1. Have you _____ the Statue of Liberty yet?
  2. We _____ gone ice-skating yet.
  3. We just _____ Chinatown.

2 Where do we put *yet* in a sentence? Where do we put *just* in a sentence?

3 We can only use *yet* with **two** of the following. Which two?
  ☐ Affirmative sentences
  ☐ Questions
  ☐ Negative sentences

▶▶ **Grammar Reference 14.2 p. 144**

3 Look at the list with a partner. Say what Rod and Marilyn have done and what they haven't done yet.

> *They went shopping on Fifth Avenue.*

> *They haven't seen the Statue of Liberty yet.*

T 14.4 Listen again and check.

PRACTICE

I just did it

1 Work with a partner. Make questions with *yet* and answers with *just*.

> *Have you called your mother yet?*

> *Yes, I just called her.*

1. called your mother
2. mail the letter
3. wash your hair
4. clean the car
5. make dinner
6. meet the new student
7. have lunch
8. give your homework to the teacher
9. finish this exercise

Check it

2 Put a check (✓) next to the correct sentence.
  1. ☐ I saw John yesterday.
     ☐ I've seen John yesterday.
  2. ☐ Did you ever ate Chinese food?
     ☐ Have you ever eaten Chinese food?
  3. ☐ Donna won $5,000 last month.
     ☐ Donna has won $5,000 last month.
  4. ☐ I've never drank champagne.
     ☐ I've never drunk champagne.
  5. ☐ Tom has ever been to Canada.
     ☐ Tom has never been to Canada.
  6. ☐ Has your sister yet had the baby?
     ☐ Has your sister had the baby yet?
  7. ☐ I haven't finished my homework yet.
     ☐ I've finished my homework yet.
  8. ☐ Did she just bought a new car?
     ☐ Did she just buy a new car?

READING AND SPEAKING
How to live to be 100

1 Who is the oldest person you know? How old is he/she? What do you know about their lives? Why do you think they have lived so long? Tell the class.

2 These words are in the texts. Write them in the correct column.

cashier	ambulance driver	heart attack	lung cancer
	stroke	secretary	admiral

Jobs	Illnesses

3 Read the introduction. Are similar facts true for your country?

How to live to be 100

More and more people are living to be 100 years old. In the United States there are more than 70,000 centenarians—10 times more than there were 40 years ago. Professor Raymond Metcalf of Princeton University believes that future generations will live even longer, to 115 years and even more. Here are the stories of 3 women who have lived to be 100.

4 Work in groups of three. Each choose a different person and read about her. Answer the questions.

 1. Where was she born?
 2. Where does she live now?
 3. What jobs has she had in her life?
 4. Did she marry and have children?
 5. Is her husband still alive?
 6. What do you learn about other people in her family?
 7. What food does she like?
 8. What activities does she like doing?

5 Work with your group. Compare the three people, using your answers.

What do you think?

• Why do you think these people have lived so long? How many reasons can you find?
• Would you like to live to be 100? Why?/Why not?

Polly Rosenbaum

Polly Rosenbaum is exactly 100 years old. She was born in the small town of Ollie, Iowa, but when she was five her family moved to Colorado. Polly's father was a teacher and he wanted his three daughters to have a good education, so Polly went to the University of Colorado and studied politics. She left the university when she was 22 and worked as a teacher. In 1939 she began working as a secretary for William George Rosenbaum, a politician in Arizona. They soon married. Unfortunately, after ten happy years together, William suddenly died of a stroke. He was 59. They didn't have any children. Polly decided to become a politician like her husband and she worked in government in Arizona until she retired 25 years ago. She says, "I like to keep busy. I love going for walks with my friends and I love cooking. I've always eaten well, lots of fruit."

Alice Patterson-Smythe

Alice Patterson-Smythe was born just over 100 years ago in Edinburgh, Scotland. She now lives in Norfolk, England. She drove ambulances in the First World War, and worked as a school secretary until she retired at age 65. She has been a widow for 25 years and has 3 children, 6 grandchildren, and 11 great-grandchildren. She smoked quite a lot when she was a young girl but she quit when she was 68 because she had a heart attack. Her nineties were the best years of her life because her millionaire grandson took her on his airplane to visit Tokyo, Los Angeles, and Miami. She says: "I love life. I play golf once a week and do Latin dancing, and I eat lots of fruit and vegetables. We are a long-lived family—my mother was 95 when she died."

Merle McEathron

Merle McEathron was 104 last July. She was born in Indiana but has lived in Phoenix, Arizona, for most of her life. She married for the first time when she was only 15 and she had 2 sons. Her husband left her when the boys were still young. Merle moved to Phoenix and became a cashier in a restaurant. At age 52, she married again, but her husband died of lung cancer only 2 years after they married. She went back to work in the restaurant and started going to dances. At one dance she finally met "the love of her life," Ellsworth McEathron, a retired admiral. She quit working at the age of 75 and at 80 got married again. They had ten beautiful years together before he too died. She says: "I still go to dances, and I might even meet another nice man. But I don't want to get married again. Now I'm happy just eating chocolates and watching TV."

LISTENING
Leaving on a jet plane

1 **T 14.5** Close your books and your eyes and listen to a song. What is it about?

2 Read the words of the song. Choose the word on the right that best completes the line.

Leaving on a Jet Plane

My (1)_____ are packed, I'm ready to go,
I'm standing here outside your (2)_____ ,
I (3)_____ to wake you up to say good-bye,
But the dawn is breaking,
It's early morn',
The taxi's (4)_____ ,
He's blowing his (5)_____ ,
Already I'm so lonesome
I could (6)_____ .

Chorus   So kiss me and (7)_____ for me,
(8)_____ me that you'll wait for me,
(9)_____ me like you'll never let me go,
'Cause I'm leaving on a jet plane,
I don't know when I'll be back again.
Oh, babe, I hate to go.

There's so (10)_____ times I've let you down,
So many times I've (11)_____ around,
I tell you now
they don't mean a thing.
Every (12)_____ I go, I'll think of you
Every song I sing, I'll sing for you
When I (13)_____ back
I'll wear your wedding (14)_____ .

1.	bags	suitcases
2.	window	door
3.	hate	want
4.	here	waiting
5.	horn	trumpet
6.	cry	die
7.	laugh	smile
8.	tell	say
9.	love	hold
10.	much	many
11.	played	walked
12.	time	place
13.	come	go
14.	ring	dress

3 Listen again and check the words. Sing along!

EVERYDAY ENGLISH
At the airport

1 What do you do at an airport? Read the sentences and put them in the correct order.

___ You wait in the departure lounge.   ___ You check in your luggage and get a boarding pass.
___ You board the plane.   ___ You go through passport control.
___ You get a cart for your luggage.   ___ You check the departures monitor for your gate number.
_1_ You arrive at the airport.

2 **T 14.6** Listen to the airport announcements and complete the chart.

FLIGHT NUMBER		DESTINATION	GATE NUMBER	REMARKS
United	8 2 3	SEATTLE	1 4	NOW BOARDING
American		LOS ANGELES		DELAYED
Northwest		DETROIT		NOW BOARDING
Air Canada		WINNIPEG		NOW BOARDING
Delta		ATLANTA		STANDBY

3 **T 14.7** Listen to the conversations. Who are the people? Where are they? Choose from these places.

- in the arrival area
- in the departure lounge
- at the departure gate
- at the check-in desk

4 Complete each conversation with the correct question.

> When can we see each other again?
> Did you have a good time in New York?
> Did they say gate 4 or 14?
> Do you have any carry-on luggage?

1. **A** Listen! ... United flight 823 to Seattle. That's our flight.
   B _____ ?
   A I couldn't hear. I think it said 14.
   B Look! There it is on the monitor. It *is* gate 14.
   A OK. Come on! Let's go.

2. **A** Can I have your ticket, please?
   B Yes, of course.
   A Thank you. How many suitcases do you have?
   B Just one.
   A _____ ?
   B Just this bag.
   A That's fine.
   B Oh ... can I have a window seat?
   A Sure ... OK. Seat 12A. Here's your boarding pass. Have a nice flight!

3. **A** Rod! Marilyn! Over here!
   B Hi! Judy! Great to see you!
   A It's great to see you, too. You look terrific! _____ ?
   B Fantastic. Everything was great.
   A Well, you haven't missed anything here. Nothing much has happened at all!

4. **A** Well, that's my flight. It's time to go.
   B It's been a wonderful two weeks. I can't believe it's over.
   A I know. _____ ?
   B Soon, I hope. I'll write every day.
   A I'll call, too. Good-bye.
   B Good-bye. Give my love to your family.

T 14.7 Listen and check. Practice the conversations with a partner.

5 Work with a partner. Make more conversations at each of the places.

Getting Information

PRACTICE
Who is he?

1 Ask and answer questions to complete the information.

RBS INTERNATIONAL **IDENTITY CARD**

LAST NAME	BINCHEY
FIRST NAME	
COUNTRY	IRELAND
JOB	
ADDRESS	82 HILL ROAD
	DUBLIN
PHONE NUMBER	
AGE	47
MARRIED?	

2 Ask and answer Yes/No questions about Patrick.
1. Smith? Jones? Binchey?
2. from the United States? from Canada? from Ireland?
3. a police officer? a teacher? an accountant?

PRACTICE
Complete your picture

1 Look at this picture of a living room. *Don't* look at your partner's picture.

2 Your picture is not complete. Ask Student B questions and find out where these things go. Draw them on your picture.

Student A Where's the lamp?
Student B It's on the table.
Student A Where exactly?
Student B It's on the table, next to the book.

3 Student B's picture is not complete. Answer Student B's questions and help him/her complete the picture.

PRACTICE

Complete your picture

1 Look at this picture of a living room. *Don't* look at your partner's picture.

2 Student A's picture is not complete. Answer Student A's questions and help him/her complete the picture.

Student A Where's the lamp?
Student B It's on the table.
Student A Where exactly?
Student B It's on the table, next to the book.

3 Your picture is not complete. Ask Student A questions and find out where these things go. Draw them on your picture.

READING AND SPEAKING
Role play

Student A You are a journalist. Complete the questions.
Student B You are Alexandra or Wesley. (You choose.) Complete the answers.

A Hello, _____ . Can I _____ you a few questions?

B Yes, of course.

A First of all, how old _____ you?

B I'm _____ .

A And do you _____ to school?

B Yes, I _____ .

A And _____ do you live?

B I live in _____ with _____ .

A Were you special when you _____ very young?

B Well, maybe. You see, I could _____ .

A Wow! That's amazing! Tell me, do you _____ much free time?

B No, I _____ , because I _____ .

A I see. And do you _____ to different countries?

B Oh, yes. Last year I _____ _____ .

A Thank you very much. That's all very interesting. Good luck in the future!

B Thanks!

Practice the interview with your partner. Then act it out in class.

EVERYDAY ENGLISH
On the phone

1 Call Directory Assistance for Noriko's phone and fax numbers. Your partner is the operator.

GENKI DESIGNS
VANCOUVER

Noriko Tanaka
85 Robson Street
Vancouver, British Columbia V6G 1B9
Canada
Tel: [   ]   Fax: [   ]
e-mail: tanaka@hotmall.com

Operator International Directory Assistance. Which country, please?
You _____ .
Operator And the city?
You _____ .
Operator Can I have the last name, please?
You _____ .
Operator And the first name?
You _____ .
Operator What's the address?
You _____ .
Recorded message The number is _____ .

2 Switch roles. You are the operator. Your partner wants Phillip's phone and fax numbers.

35 Market Street
Atlanta, GA 30324
USA
e-mail: PWPaulson@yoohoo.com
Tel: **(404) 555-6061**
Fax: **(404) 555-9462**

Phillip W. Paulson

FAMOUS INVENTIONS
Getting information

When were these things invented? Ask and answer questions about the exact dates when these things were invented. Write down the dates. How many years ago was it?

A When was Coca-Cola invented?
B In 1893.
A Hmm. That was _____ years ago.

1. Coca-Cola was invented in _____ .
2. The camera was invented in 1826.
3. The record player was invented in _____ .
4. The first plane was invented in 1903.
5. Jeans were invented in _____ .
6. Hamburgers were invented in 1895.
7. Cars were invented in _____ .
8. The telephone was invented in 1876.
9. The television was invented in _____ .
10. Bicycles were invented in about 1810.

FAMOUS INVENTIONS
Getting information

When were these things invented? Ask and answer questions about the exact dates when these things were invented. Write down the dates. How many years ago was it?

    A When was Coca-Cola invented?

    B In 1893.

    A Hmm. That was _____ years ago.

1. Coca-Cola was invented in 1886.
2. The camera was invented in _____ .
3. The record player was invented in 1878.
4. The first plane was invented in _____ .
5. Jeans were invented in 1873.
6. Hamburgers were invented in _____ .
7. Cars were invented in 1893.
8. The telephone was invented in _____ .
9. The television was invented in 1926.
10. Bicycles were invented in about _____ .

PRACTICE
Did you know that ... ?

1 Read this incredible information to Student B.

Did you know that ... ?

Really? That's incredible!

No way! I don't believe it!

Well, it's true!

The painter Vincent van Gogh sold only two paintings while he was alive.

The Empire State Building has 6,400 windows.

King Louis XIV of France had a bath only three times in his life.

There are almost 1,000 tornadoes in the United States each year.

2 Listen to Student B's incredible information and respond.

The Mona Lisa

The Great Wall of China

Walt Disney

The Sahara Desert

PRACTICE
Did you know that ... ?

1 Listen to Student A's incredible information and respond.

Did you know that ... ?

Really? That's incredible!

No way! I don't believe it!

Well, it's true!

Vincent van Gogh

The Empire State Building

King Louis XIV of France

A tornado

2 Read your incredible information to Student A.

King Francis I of France bought the painting the *Mona Lisa* to put in his bathroom.

It took 1,700 years to build the Great Wall of China.

Walt Disney used his own voice for the character of Mickey Mouse.

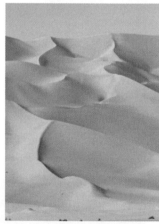

In 1979 it snowed in the Sahara Desert.

PRACTICE

Who's at the party?

You and your partner have different pictures of the same party. There are ten differences! Talk about the pictures to find them. *Don't* look at your partner's picture.

In my picture three people are dancing.

In my picture four people are dancing.

There's a girl with blonde hair.

Is she wearing a black dress?

PRACTICE

Who's at the party?

You and your partner have different pictures of the same party. There are ten differences! Talk about the pictures to find them. *Don't* look at your partner's picture.

In my picture three people are dancing.

In my picture four people are dancing.

There's a girl with blonde hair.

Is she wearing a black dress?

VOCABULARY AND SPEAKING
World weather

3 Ask and answer questions to complete the information.

WORLD WEATHER:

		°C
Atlanta	S	30
Boston	C	18
Brasilia	—	—
Denver	C	16
Hong Kong	—	—
London	Fg	15
Los Angeles		
Mexico City	S	25
San Francisco	—	—
São Paolo	S	25
Seattle	—	—
Toronto	C	16
Vancouver	—	—

S = sunny
C = cloudy
Fg = foggy
R = rainy
Sn = snowy

4 Which city was the hottest? Which was the coldest? Which month do you think it is?

EVERYDAY ENGLISH
Catching a train

DEPARTURE TIME New York	ARRIVAL TIME Philadelphia
6:00 A.M.	7:22 A.M.
8:05 A.M.	8:45 A.M.
10:25 A.M.	11:54 A.M.
5:09 P.M.	6:27 P.M.
7:20 P.M.	8:10 P.M.
9:24 P.M.	10:35 P.M.
Round trip $79.00	

DEPARTURE TIME New York	ARRIVAL TIME Washington, D.C.
6:08 A.M.	9:52 A.M.
8:00 A.M.	10:59 A.M.
9:20 A.M.	12:45 P.M.
5:50 P.M.	8:49 P.M.
6:15 P.M.	9:52 P.M.
8:31 P.M.	11:55 P.M.
Round trip $115.00	

DEPARTURE TIME New York	ARRIVAL TIME Providence
6:58 A.M.	11:12 A.M.
8:35 A.M.	12:49 P.M.
10:44 A.M.	1:57 P.M.
4:55 P.M.	8:06 P.M.
6:05 P.M.	10:21 P.M.
7:32 P.M.	11:40 P.M.
Round trip $99.00	

EVERYDAY ENGLISH
On the phone

1 You are the operator. Your partner wants Noriko's phone and fax numbers.

GENKI DESIGNS
VANCOUVER

Noriko Tanaka
85 Robson Street
Vancouver, British Columbia V6G 1B9
Canada
Tel: (604) 555-8142   Fax: (604) 555-8143
e-mail: tanaka@hotmall.com

Operator	International Directory Assistance. Which country, please?
You	_____ .
Operator	And the city?
You	_____ .
Operator	Can I have the last name, please?
You	_____ .
Operator	And the first name?
You	_____ .
Operator	What's the address?
You	_____ .
Recorded message	The number is _____ .

2 Switch roles. Call Directory Assistance for Phillip's phone and fax numbers. Your partner is the operator.

35 Market Street
Atlanta, GA 30324
USA
e-mail: PWPaulson@yoohoo.com
Tel:
Fax:

Phillip W. Paulson

Tapescripts

Unit 1

T 1.1 see p. 2

T 1.2

A Hello. My name's Gordon. What's your name?
B Jun.
A Where are you from, Jun?
B I'm from Seoul, South Korea. Where are you from?
A I'm from Toronto, Canada.

T 1.3 see p. 3

T 1.4 Listen carefully

1. He's from Taiwan.
2. What's her name?
3. They're from Brazil.
4. Where's she from?
5. He's a teacher in Italy.

T 1.5 see p. 3

T 1.6 Yaling

My name's Yaling Chen and I'm a student. I am 19. I'm not married. I have one sister and two brothers. I live in an apartment in Taipei, Taiwan. I want to learn English because it's an international language.

T 1.7 The alphabet song

A B C D E F G,
H I J K L M N O P,
Q R S, T U V,
W X Y and Z

T 1.8 see p. 6

T 1.9 Telephone numbers

726-9304
919-677-1303
1-800-445-9714

T 1.10 What are the numbers?

1. My brother has four children.
2. I have 10 stamps in my wallet.
3. I live at 19 Hudson Street.
4. Good-bye. See you at 5.
5. Hello. This is 428-0261. Please leave a message.
6. Please call me. My number is 625-4673.

T 1.11 Everyday conversations

1. Hello. Marty Freeman.
   Hi, Marty. It's Jane. How are you?
   I'm fine, thanks. And you?
   Pretty good, thanks.

2. Is 7 o'clock OK with you, Bianca?
   Yes. Seven is fine.
   OK. See you then. Good-bye.
   Good-bye, Michael.

3. Hello?
   Hi, Flora! It's me, Leo. How are you?
   Not bad, thanks. How are you?
   Just fine. How are the children?
   They're fine.

Unit 2

T 2.1 Keesha Anderson

1. A What's her last name?
   B Anderson.
2. A What's her first name?
   B Keesha.
3. A Where's she from?
   B The United States.
4. A What's her job?
   B She's a journalist.
5. A What's her address?
   B 71 Canyon Drive, Los Angeles, California.
6. A What's her phone number?
   B (310) 440-7305.
7. A How old is she?
   B Twenty-eight.
8. A Is she married?
   B No, she isn't.

T 2.2 Daniel Anderson

A What's his last name?
B Anderson.
A What's his first name?
B Daniel.
A Where's he from?
B The United States.
A What's his job?
B He's a police officer.
A What's his address?
B 655 Thomas Street, San Francisco, California.
A What's his phone number?
B It's (415) 753-7080.
A How old is he?
B He's 26.
A Is he married?
B No, he isn't.

T 2.3 see p. 9

T 2.4 see p. 10

T 2.5 Adjectives

1. He's old. She's young.
2. It's easy. It's difficult.
3. It's new. It's old.
4. It's fast. It's slow.
5. It's nice. It's awful.
6. They're hot. They're cold.
7. They're cheap. They're expensive.
8. It's small. It's big.

T 2.6 see p. 13

T 2.7 Dorita in New York

D = Dorita   K = Kenji
1. D Hello. My name's Dorita.
   K Hello, Dorita. I'm Kenji.
   D Where are you from?
   K I'm from Osaka—Osaka, Japan. And you? Where are you from?
   D I'm from Argentina.
   K From Buenos Aires?
   D Yes, that's right.

I = Isabel   C = class   D = Dorita
2. I Good morning, everybody.
   C Good morning, Isabel.
   I How are you all?
   C Fine.
      Good.
      OK.
   I How are you, Dorita?
   D I'm fine, thank you. And you?
   I Very well, thank you. Now, listen everybody, because I want to tell you…

M = Marnie   A = Annie   D = Dorita
3. M Bye, Dorita. Have a nice day.
   D Pardon?
   A Have a good day at English school.
   D Ah, yes …. Thank you. Same to you.
   M What's your teacher called?
   D My teacher … called?
   A Your teacher's name—what is it?
   D Ah, yes. Her name's Isabel.
   M And is she good?
   D My teacher … uh, … good?
   A Yeah, Isabel. Your teacher … is she a good teacher?
   D Oh, yes, yes. Very good, very nice.

T 2.8 see p. 14

T 2.9 Prices

1. That's 5 dollars and 50 cents, please.
2. You can buy it for only ten dollars.
3. Here's 25 cents.
4. A grilled chicken sandwich is only three-ninety.
5. A hundred dollars for that is very expensive!
6. That's seven-*fifty*, not seven-*fifteen*.

T 2.11   **In a cafe**

A   Good morning.
B   Good morning. Can I have an orange juice, please?
A   Sure. Anything else?
B   No thanks.
A   A dollar-fifty, please.
B   Here you go.
A   Thank you.

A   Hi. Can I help you?
B   Yes. Can I have a tuna salad sandwich, please?
A   Anything to drink?
B   Yeah. A mineral water, please.
A   OK. Here you are.
B   Thanks. How much is that?
A   Four seventy-five, please.
B   OK. Thanks.

Unit 3

T 3.1   see p. 16

T 3.2

1. He's a computer scientist. She's a doctor.
2. David comes from Taiwan. Pam comes from Canada.
3. She lives in a big city, but he lives in a small town.
4. He works 3 days a week. She works 16 hours a day nonstop.
5. She speaks to sick people on her radio. He speaks 3 languages.
6. She loves her job and he loves his job, too.
7. He has a daughter. She isn't married.
8. He likes playing tennis and riding his bicycle in his free time. She never has free time.

T 3.3   **Questions and answers**

Where does David come from? Taipei, in Taiwan.
What does he do? He's a computer scientist.
Does he speak Chinese? Yes, he does.
Does he speak Spanish? No, he doesn't.

T 3.4

1. Where does Pam come from? Canada.
2. What does she do? She's a doctor.
3. Does she fly to help people? Yes, she does.
4. Does she speak Chinese and Japanese? No, she doesn't.

T 3.5   **Is it true or false?**

1. Fernando comes from Brazil.
2. Fernando lives in New York.
3. Fernando works all over Fortaleza.
4. Fernando speaks English very well.
5. Fernando's married.
6. Keiko lives and works in New York.

7. Keiko speaks French and German.
8. Keiko plays tennis in her free time.
9. Keiko isn't married.
10. Mark works in an office in Moscow.
11. Mark has three sons.
12. Mark likes playing soccer in his free time.

T 3.6   **Listen carefully**

1. She likes her job.
2. She loves walking.
3. He isn't married.
4. Does he have three children?
5. What does he do?

T 3.7   **Mr. McSporran's day**

1. A   Good afternoon. Can I have two ice creams, please?
   B   Chocolate or vanilla?
   A   One chocolate, one vanilla, please.
   B   That's £1.80. Anything else?
   A   No, thank you.
2. A   Only two letters for you this morning, Mrs. Craig.
   B   Thank you very much, Mr. McSporran. And how's Mrs. McSporran this morning?
   A   Oh, she's very well, thank you. She's busy in the shop.
3. A   A glass of wine before bed, my dear?
   B   Oh, yes please.
   A   Here you are.
   B   Thank you, my dear. I'm very tired this evening.
4. A   Hello, Mr. McSporran.
   B   Good morning, boys and girls. Hurry up, we're late!
   A   Can I sit here, Mr. McSporran?
   C   No, no, I want to sit there.
   B   Be quiet all of you, and SIT DOWN!

T 3.8   **What time is it?**

It's five o'clock.
It's eight o'clock.
It's five-thirty.
It's eleven thirty.
It's a quarter after five.
It's a quarter after two.
It's a quarter to six.
It's a quarter to nine.
It's five after five.
It's ten after five.
It's twenty after five.
It's twenty-five after five.
It's twenty-five to six.
It's twenty to six.
It's ten to six.
It's five to six.

T 3.9   see p. 23

Unit 4

T 4.1   **Bobbi Brown's weekdays**

My weekends are busy and exciting. My weekdays at home are busy, too! I have two sons, Dylan, 7, and Dakota, 5. Every morning I get up one hour before them, at 6, and I go to the gym. I come home and I make breakfast. Then I take them to school. On Mondays I always go shopping. I buy all the food for the week. I often cook dinner in the evenings, but not every day because I don't like cooking. Fortunately, my husband, Don, loves cooking. On Tuesdays and Thursdays I visit my father. He lives on the next block. Every afternoon I pick up the kids from school. In the evenings Don and I usually relax, but sometimes we visit friends. We never go out on Friday evenings because I start work so early on Saturdays.

T 4.2   **Questions and answers**

B = Bobbi
A   Where do you work?
B   In New York.
A   Do you like your work?
B   Yes, I do.
A   Do you relax on weekends?
B   No, I don't.
A   Why don't you relax on weekends?
B   Because I work.

T 4.3

1. What time do you go to bed?
   At 11 o'clock.
2. Where do you go on vacation?
   To Hawaii or California.
3. What do you do on Sundays?
   I always relax.
4. When do you do your homework?
   After dinner.
5. Who do you live with?
   My mother and sisters.
6. Why do you like your job?
   Because it's interesting.
7. How do you travel to school?
   By bus.
8. Do you go out on Friday evenings?
   Yes, I do sometimes.

T 4.4   **Listen carefully**

1. What does she do on Sundays?
2. Do you stay home on Thursday evenings?
3. He lives here.
4. What do you do on Saturday evenings?
5. I read a lot.
6. Why don't you like your job?

T 4.5   see pp. 28–29

T 4.6

M = Marisol   J = Jane   F = Marisol's friends

1. **M** Hello, everybody! This is my friend
       Jane from Seattle.
    F Hi!
    F Hello!
    F Hello, Jane!
    J Hello. It's nice to meet you.
    M Sit down here, Jane.
    J Thanks.
    F Do you like the music, Jane?
    J Yes, I do. Where's it from?
    F It's from Cuba!

T = Toshi   A = Ann

2. **T** Hello, Mrs. Jones. I'm pleased to meet
       you.
    A I'm pleased to meet you, too.
    T Please come in. You're from our office
       in Los Angeles, aren't you?
    A Yes, that's right.
    T Welcome to Tokyo! Do you like our
       headquarters here?
    A Yes. It's very big. How many people
       work here?
    T About 6,000 people. Would you like to
       see our offices?

A = Al   M = Michael

3. **A** Well, what do you want to do today,
       Michael?
    M Ooh, I don't know. What about you?
    A Do you like sailing?
    M Yes, very much.
    A OK—so today let's go sailing and
       fishing on the lake.
    M Great! I love fishing, too!

T 4.7 Everyday conversations

1. **A** I'm sorry I'm late. The traffic is bad
       today.
    B That's OK. Come and sit down. We're
       on page 35.
2. **A** Excuse me.
    B Yes?
    A Do you have a pencil?
    B I'm sorry, I only have a pen.
    A Oh, OK. Thanks anyway.
3. **A** It's very hot in here. Can I open the
       window?
    B Really? I'm kind of cold.
    A OK. It doesn't matter.
4. **A** Excuse me.
    B Can I help you?
    A Can I have some film for my camera?
    B How many exposures?
    A Pardon?
    B How many exposures?
    A What does "exposures" mean?
    B How many pictures? 24? 36?
    A Ah! Now I understand! Twenty-four,
       please.

Unit 5

T 5.1 Questions and answers

A Is there a television?
B Yes, there is.
A Is there a radio?
B No, there isn't.
A Are there any books?
B Yes, there are.
A How many books are there?
B There are a lot.
A Are there any photographs?
B No, there aren't.

T 5.2 Description of a living room

There are three people in the living room—a
man and a woman on the sofa and a little girl
in the armchair.
There's a radio on the coffee table and a rug
under it.
There's a cat on the rug in front of the
armchair.
There are a lot of pictures on the walls but
there aren't any photographs.
There are two plants on the floor next to the
television and some flowers on the small table
next to the sofa.

T 5.3 Helen's kitchen

H = Helen   B = Bob

H …And this is the kitchen.
B Wow … it's really nice.
H Well, it's not very big, but there are a lot of
    cabinets. And there's a new refrigerator,
    and an oven. That's new, too.
B But what's *in* all these cabinets?
H Well, not a lot. There are some cups, but
    there aren't any plates. And I have some
    knives and forks, but I don't have any
    spoons!
B Do you have any glasses?
H No, I don't.
B That's OK. We can drink this champagne
    from those cups! Cheers!

T 5.4 What's in Yoshi's briefcase?

What's in my briefcase? Well, there's a
newspaper—a Japanese newspaper—and
there's a dictionary—my Japanese/English
dictionary. I have some pens, three I think.
Also, I have a notebook for vocabulary. I write
words in that every day. And of course I have
my keys—my car keys and my house keys.
And, oh yes, very important, there are some
photos of my family—my wife and my
daughter. That's all I think. I don't have any
stamps or envelopes and my address book is
in my hotel.

T 5.5 Homes around the world

1. Manola from Lisbon
I live in the old town near the sea. It is called
"the Alfama." I have a very beautiful
apartment. There's just one room in my
apartment, one very big room with one very
big window. My bed's next to the window so I

see the sea and all the lights of the city when I
go to sleep. I live alone, but I have a cat and
I'm near the stores and lots of friends come to
visit me. I love my apartment.

2. Ray and Elsie from Toronto
Elsie Our house is pretty old—about 50
       years old—and it's near the city center.
       We have a living room, a big kitchen,
       and, uh, three bedrooms, but the room
       we love is our family room.
Ray Yes. There's a TV and a stereo and a
       large comfortable sofa in there, and
       some big, old armchairs. We love sitting
       there in winter with the snow outside.
Elsie Our children aren't at home now. They
       both have jobs in the U.S., so most of
       the time it's just Ray and me.

3. Brad from Malibu
My house is fantastic. It's right next to the
ocean. I have a lot of rich neighbors—some of
them are famous actors. My house has ten
rooms, and five are bedrooms. Almost
everything in my house is white—the floors,
the walls, the sofas, the carpets …. I also have
a swimming pool, a private screening room
for movies, and an exercise room. I live here
alone. I'm not married at the moment. My ex-
wife is French. She lives in Paris now with our
three sons.

4. Alise from Samoa
I live with my family in a house near the sea.
We have an open house—ummm—that is—
our house doesn't have any walls. Houses in
Samoa don't have walls because it's very, very
hot, but we have blinds to stop the rain and
sun. Our house is in the old style. We have
only one room for living and sleeping, so it is
both a bedroom and a living room. We have
rugs and we sit and sleep on the floor.

T 5.6 Asking for directions

1. **A** Excuse me. Is there a drugstore near
       here?
    B Yes. It's over there.
    A Thanks.
2. **A** Excuse me. Is there a newsstand near
       here?
    B Yes. It's on Davis Street. Just go straight
       and then turn right on Davis. It's next
       to the music store.
    A OK. Thanks.
3. **A** Excuse me. Is there a restaurant near
       here?
    B There's a Chinese one on Maple Street,
       next to the bank, and there's an Italian
       one on Davis Street next to the post
       office.
    A Is that one far?
    B No. It's just a block away. It takes two
       minutes, that's all.
4. **A** Is there a post office near here?
    B Go straight ahead. It's on the left, next
       to the Italian restaurant.
    A Thanks a lot.

Unit 6

T 6.1 **What can you do?**
a. 2. She can use a computer.
b. 6. We can't understand the question.
c. 3. Can dogs swim? Yes, they can.
d. 1. He can ski really well.
e. 5. I can't spell your name.
f. 4. Can you speak Japanese? No, I can't.

T 6.2. **Listen and repeat.**
I can speak Spanish.
Can you speak Spanish?
Yes, I can.
No, I can't.

T 6.3 **Listen and complete the sentences.**
1. I can speak French, but I can't speak Korean.
2. He can't dance, but he can sing.
3. Can you cook? Yes, I can.
4. They can ski, but they can't swim.
5. We can dance and we can sing.
6. Can she drive? No, she can't.

T 6.4 **Tina can't cook. Can you?**
Well, there are a lot of things I can't do. I can't drive a car, but I want to take driving lessons soon. I can't speak French, but I can speak Spanish—my mother's Mexican, and we often go to Mexico to visit her family. My mother's a good cook. She can cook really well, not just Mexican food—all kinds of food. But I can't cook at all. I just love eating! What about sports? Well … I think I'm good at a lot of sports. I can play tennis, and of course I can swim, but I can't ski. But musical instruments—no. I can't play any at all. I'm not very musical, but I love dancing! Of course I can use a computer—all my friends can.

T 6.5 **Listen and repeat.**
It was Monday yesterday. We were at school.
Was it hot? Yes, it was.
Were you tired? Yes, we were.

T 6.6 **Carol's party**
K = Kim   M = Max
K Were you at Carol's party last Saturday?
M Yes, I was.
K Was it good?
M Well, it was OK.
K Were there many people?
M Yes, there were.
K Was Henry there?
M No, he wasn't. And where were you? Why weren't you there?
K Oh,… I couldn't go because I was at Mark's party! It was great!

T 6.7 **Directory Assistance**
Operator International Directory Assistance. Which country, please?
Operator And the city?
Operator Can I have the last name, please?
Operator And the first name?
Operator What's the address?
Recorded message The number is: 0 1 1 6 1 9 8 4 6 8 1 1 3 3.

T 6.8 **On the phone**
1. A Hello.
   B Hello. Can I speak to Gina, please?
   A This is Gina.
   B Oh! Hi, Gina. This is Pat. Is Sunday still OK for tennis?
   A Yes. That's fine.
   B Great! See you on Sunday at ten. Bye!
   A Bye!
2. A Hello.
   B Hello. Is this Liz?
   A No, it isn't. Hold on … I'll get her.
   C Hello, this is Liz.
   B Hi, Liz. It's Tom. Listen. There's a party at my house on Saturday. Can you come?
   C Oh, I'm sorry, but I can't. It's my sister's wedding.
   B That's OK. Maybe next time. Bye!
   C Bye!
3. A Good morning. Bank One. How can I help you?
   B Good morning. Can I speak to the manager, please?
   A I'm afraid Mr. Smith isn't in his office at the moment. Can I take a message?
   B No, that's OK. I'll call again later.
   A All right. Good-bye.
   B Good-bye.

Unit 7

T 7.1 **Mattie Smith**
Mattie Smith is 91 years old. She lives alone in Atlanta, Georgia. She starts her day at 7:30. First she takes a bath, next she cleans the house, and then she sits outside on her front porch and thinks about her past life. Then she writes poems about it.

T 7.2 see p. 48

T 7.3 **Listen and repeat.**
looked
worked
loved
learned
earned
married
died
hated
wanted

T 7.4 **Listen to Mattie.**
I worked all day, from morning until night. Twelve hours in the cotton fields and I only earned $4 a day. I sure hated that job—but I loved the poems in my head. I really wanted to learn to read and write.
    When I was 16 I married Hubert, and soon there were 6 children: 5 sons, then a daughter, Lily. Hubert died just before she was born. That was 65 years ago. So I looked after my family alone.
    There was no time for learning, but my children, they all learned to read and write. That was important to me.
    And when did I learn to read and write? I didn't learn until I was 86, and now I have 3 books of poems.

T 7.5 **Questions and answers**
1. A When did she start to work?
   B When she was eight years old.
2. A Where did she work?
   B In the cotton fields.
3. A Who did she live with?
   B Her mother and sisters.
4. A How many hours did she work?
   B Twelve hours a day.
5. A How much did she earn?
   B Four dollars a day.
6. A Who did she marry?
   B Hubert.
7. A When did Hubert die?
   B Sixty-five years ago.
8. A When did she learn to read?
   B She didn't learn until she was 86.

T 7.6 **Listen carefully**
worked
lived
started
married
loved
hated
finished
looked
earned
visited
cleaned
liked

T 7.7 **Listen and repeat.**
had
left
won
fought
got
lost
studied
bought
went
became
met
died

T 7.8 Steve's 1990s

What do I remember about the nineties? …
Ummm, well, I left home in 1993 and went to
college. I studied economics—it was really
interesting. I had a good time. Then after
college, in 1997, I was really lucky. I got a job
immediately, at Chase Manhattan Bank, a big
bank in New York. Soon after that, in 1998, I
met my wife, Gail. We got married in 1999
and bought a nice house together. We're very
happy now.

Well, basketball is OK … but I really love
soccer. I remember that in 1994, the Soccer
World Cup was in the United States. Brazil
won in 1994. In 1998, the World Cup was in
France. That year, Brazil lost to France.

Well, the U.S. fought in the Gulf War in
1991. Bill Clinton became president in 1992.
He was president for eight years—from 1992
to 2000. I'll never forget the presidential
election in 2000, because we had a lot of
problems.

One thing I remember about 1997 that
was really sad was when Princess Diana died.
She died in a car crash in Paris—I remember
it was on the news for days.

T 7.9 see p. 54

T 7.10 see p. 54

T 7.11 Listen and repeat.

1. bought
2. could
3. night
4. answer
5. island
6. Christmas

T 7.12 see p. 54

T 7.13 Special days

1. **A** Ugh! Work again! I hate Monday
      mornings!
   B Me, too. Did you have a nice weekend?
   A Yes. It was great.

2. Happy birthday to you.
   Happy birthday to you.
   Happy birthday, dear Tommy,
   Happy birthday to you.

3. **A** Did you get any Valentine's Day cards?
   B Yes, I did. Listen to this.
      Roses are red. Violets are blue
      You are my Valentine
      And I love you.
   A Oooh! Do you know who it's from?
   B No idea!

4. **A** Congratulations!
   B Oh … thank you very much.
   A When's the happy day?
   B Excuse me?
   A Your wedding day. When is it?
   B Oh! We're not sure. Probably some
      time in June.

5. **A** It's midnight! Happy New Year
      everybody!
   B Happy New Year!
   C Happy New Year!

6. **A** Thank goodness! It's Friday!
   B Yeah. Have a nice weekend!
   A Same to you.

T 7.14 Listen and answer.

1. Did you have a nice weekend?
2. Did you get any Valentine's Day cards?
3. Congratulations!
4. Happy New Year!
5. Have a nice weekend!

Unit 8

T 8.1 Inventions

JEANS
Two Americans, Jacob Davis and Levi Strauss,
made the first jeans in 1873. Davis bought
cloth from Levi's shop. He told Levi that he
had a special way to make strong clothing for
workmen. The first jeans were blue. In 1935
jeans became fashionable for women after
they saw them in Vogue magazine. In the
1970s, Calvin Klein earned $12.5 million a
week from jeans.

TELEVISION
A Scotsman, John Logie Baird, transmitted the
first television picture on October 25, 1925.
The first thing on television was a boy who
worked in the office next to Baird's workroom
in London. In 1927, Baird sent pictures from
London to Glasgow. In 1928 he sent pictures
to New York, and also produced the first color
TV pictures.

ASPIRIN
Felix Hofman, a 29-year-old chemist who
worked for the German company Bayer,
invented the drug aspirin in March 1899. He
gave the first aspirin to his father for his
arthritis. By 1950 it was the best-selling
painkiller in the world, and in 1969 the Apollo
astronauts took it to the moon. The Spanish
philosopher José Ortega y Gassett called the
20th century "The Age of Aspirin."

T 8.2 Listen and check.

1. Two Germans didn't make the first jeans.
   Two Americans made them.
2. Davis didn't sell cloth in Levi's shop. He
   bought cloth from Levi's shop.
3. Women didn't see pictures of jeans in *She*
   magazine. They saw them in *Vogue*.
4. Baird didn't send pictures from London to
   Paris. He sent pictures from London to
   Glasgow.
5. Felix Hofman didn't give the first aspirin
   to his mother. He gave it to his father.
6. A Spanish philosopher didn't call the 19th
   century "The Age of Aspirin." He called the
   20th century "The Age of Aspirin."

T 8.3 see p. 58

T 8.4 Listen and repeat.

1. recipe
2. green
3. clock
4. banana
5. funny
6. worried
7. delicious
8. kissed

T 8.5 Listen and check.

1. **A** Why didn't you laugh at my joke?
   B Because it wasn't very funny. That's
      why!

2. **A** Hello. Hello. I can't hear you. Who is it?
   B It's me, Jonathan … JONATHAN! I'm
      on my cell phone.
   A Oh, Jonathan! Hi! Sorry, I can't talk
      now. I'm in a hurry.

3. **A** Good luck on your exams!
   B Oh, thank you. I always get so nervous
      before exams.

4. **A** Mmmmm! Did you make this
      chocolate cake?
   B I did. Do you like it?
   A Like it? I love it. It's delicious. Can I
      have the recipe?

5. **A** Come on, Tommy. Say hello to your
      Aunt Mavis. Don't be shy.
   B Hello, Aunt Mavis.

T 8.6

Love on the Internet: Marie and Chris
C = Chris   M = Marie
M I'm really shy. I find it difficult to talk to
   people face to face. But I find it easy to
   chat on the Internet. I met Chris there
   about a year ago. It was in a chat room
   called "the Chat Room." He was so funny.
C But I'm only funny on the Internet!
   Anyway, we "chatted" on the Internet for a
   year, we exchanged hundreds of e-mails
   and some photos. I wanted to call Marie
   but—
M I said no. I was worried. I didn't want it to
   end.
C She didn't even give me her address. But
   finally she said OK, I could call. So I did,
   and we spoke for an hour. That was six
   months ago. Then she sent me her address
   and …
M …that was three months ago and one
   week later, there was a knock at the door
   and I knew before I opened it. Somehow I
   wasn't worried anymore. I opened the
   door and …
C …and I stood there with some flowers …
M …lots of flowers. Red roses. Beautiful …
   and …
C …and well, we fell in love and …
Both   …and we got married last Saturday!

Love in a bottle: Yuko and Vince

Y = Yuko   V = Vince

Y I love the sea. I like walking on the beach. One day, it was five years ago now, I was on the beach and I stood on something. It was a bottle, a green bottle. I could see something inside—some paper. So I broke the bottle, it was a letter but …

V …but you couldn't read it …

Y No, I couldn't. You see it was in English and I couldn't speak English then.

V You can speak it very well now…

Y No, not really … but anyway. I asked a friend to translate the letter for me. We couldn't believe it. A man in Alaska wanted a wife, but the letter was ten years old.

V And I still wasn't married!

Y But I didn't know that. Anyway for a joke, my friend and I wrote a letter and sent a photo…

V And now, I couldn't believe it. I got this letter and a photo. She was beautiful. I wrote back immediately and we wrote every week for six months … and we spoke on the phone and …

Y …and finally I flew to Anchorage, way up north in Alaska, and we met face to face. I was very shy but it was good, very good and now …

V …now, we have 3 children. We have a house by the sea…

Y We're very happy. You see, we both love the sea!

T 8.7 Ordinals

first
second
third
fourth
fifth
sixth
tenth
twelfth
thirteenth
sixteenth
seventeenth
twentieth
twenty-first
thirtieth
thirty-first

T 8.8 Dates

1. April first
2. March second
3. September seventeenth
4. November nineteenth
5. June twenty-third
6. February twenty-ninth, 1976
7. December nineteenth, 1983
8. October third, 1999
9. May thirty-first, 2000
10. July fifteenth, two thousand four

T 8.9 What's the date?

1. January fourth
2. May seventh, 1997
3. August fifteenth, 2001
4. **A** It was a Friday.
   B No, it wasn't. It was a Thursday.
   A No, I remember. It was Friday the 13th. July 13th.
5. **A** Oh, no! I forgot your birthday.
   B It doesn't matter, really.
   A It was last Sunday, wasn't it? The 30th. November 30th.
6. **B** Hey! Did you know that Shakespeare was born and died on the same day?
   A That's not possible!
   B Yes, it is. He was born on April 23, 1564, and he died on April 23, 1616.

Unit 9

T 9.1 Food you like

D = Donna   T = Tom

D I don't like tea.

T Oh, I do… Sometimes I have it with milk and sugar. But coffee's terrible!

D Yeah. Disgusting. I don't like it either.

T But I like soda … and apple juice, too.

D Yeah. I really like apple juice. It's delicious.

T Yeah, and it's good for you. Apples are too … I love all fruit—apples, oranges, bananas, strawberries …

D Yeah. I like fruit, but I hate all vegetables, especially tomatoes.

T Yeah, vegetables are disgusting. But not all of them—I really like peas and carrots. Hamburgers, french fries, and carrot sticks. *Mmm*! That's one of my favorite meals.

D Yeah—hamburgers, I like. French fries, I like. But carrots? Yuck!

T My favorite meal is spaghetti. Spaghetti, then ice cream for dessert. Yum! Or yogurt. I love strawberry yogurt.

D Ice cream OK, yes. Yogurt, no! Spaghetti—yes. I like all pasta—and pizza! But I don't like it with tomatoes or cheese. I don't like tomatoes very much. And I hate cheese!

T *Mmmm*! Pizza is the best. But you can't have pizza without cheese!

D Yes, you can.

T No, you can't!

D Can!

T Can't!

D Well, I can. I don't like cheese at all!

T Well, what <u>do</u> you like?

D Well, I like—umm—I like chocolate, and chocolate ice cream, and chocolate chip cookies.

T So do I. Everybody likes chocolate stuff.

D Yeah!

T 9.2 see p. 63

T 9.2 see p. 63

T 9.3 Questions and answers

1. Would you like a cigarette?
   No, thanks. I don't smoke.
2. Do you like your teacher?
   Yes. She's very nice.
3. Would you like a drink?
   Yes. I'd like a soda, please.
4. Can I help you?
   Yes. I'd like a book of stamps, please.
5. What sports do you like?
   Well, I like swimming very much.
6. Excuse me, are you ready to order?
   Yes. I'd like a hamburger, please.

T 9.4 Listen carefully

1. Good afternoon. Can I help you?
2. Who's your favorite writer?
3. What would you like for your birthday?
4. Do you like animals?
5. Do you like wine?
6. Would you like some strawberries with your ice cream?

T 9.5

1. **A** Good afternoon. Can I help you?
   B Yes. I'd like some fruit, please.
2. **A** Who's your favorite writer?
   B I like books by John Grisham.
3. **A** What would you like for your birthday?
   B I'd like a new bike.
4. **A** Do you like animals?
   B I like cats, but I don't like dogs.
5. **A** Do you like wine?
   B I like French wine, especially red wine.
6. **A** Would you like some strawberries with your ice cream?
   B No, thanks. I don't like strawberries.

T 9.6 Going shopping

MB = Mrs. Bloom   B = Barry

MB Good morning. Can I help you?

B Yes. I'd like some orange juice, please.

MB Oh, I'm sorry. There's apple juice but no orange juice.

B Then what's that … ?

MB Excuse me?

B There. Isn't that orange juice?

MB Oh, yes. So it is! My eyes! Here you are.

B Thank you. And I'd like some milk, please.

MB I'm sorry. I sold the last carton two minutes ago.

B Hmmm … OK … How about some coffee?

MB All right. Yes. Here you are.

B Thanks. Let's see … orange juice, coffee, and … ummm, what else? … Oh! Apples! I'd like some apples, please.

MB I don't sell apples.

B What? No apples? That's strange. What about cheese? Can I have some cheese, please? Say, about two …

MB I don't sell cheese either.

B You don't sell cheese? I can't believe it! Well, I want some pizza, but I'm sure you don't sell pizza.

MB Oh, yes. Yes, I do. What kind of pizza would you like? There's pizza with mushrooms, pizza with ham, pizza with sausage, or pizza with tomatoes.

B Wow! That's great! Can I have … pizza with tomatoes, please?

MB Oh.

B What?

MB I forgot … Usually I have pizza. But not on Thursdays. And today's Thursday …

B Hmm. Yes. Yes, it is … S-o-o …

MB So, no pizza.

B Well, then … forget about the pizza … What about bread?

MB Bread?

B Bread. What about bread? I don't suppose you have any bread.

MB Yes. You're right.

B Excuse me?

MB You're right. There isn't any bread.

B Tell me. Do you do a lot of business?

MB Oh, yes. We're open every day!

B Really? And what do people buy?

MB All the things you see here.

B Hmmm. OK. That's all for me. How much?

MB That's $8.50.

B Thank you. Good-bye.

MB Good-bye. See you again soon.

B I don't think so.

T 9.7 My favorite food

George
Now, in my job, I travel all around the world and I like all kinds of food … but my favorite is a real American breakfast. I always have it as soon as I come home. Eggs, pancakes, bacon, and lots of coffee. Not every day, but when I'm home I like to have a big breakfast on Sunday morning. Mmmm-mmmm-mmmm.

Amy
Well, I love vegetables, all vegetables—I eat meat, too—but not much. I think that's why I like Chinese food so much. There are lots of vegetables in Chinese food. Yes, Chinese is my favorite kind of food. I can use chopsticks. Can you?

Greg
Mexican food. I love spicy food. Most Friday nights I go out with friends from work. We go to the Cantina—that's my favorite Mexican restaurant. I almost always have the enchiladas. They're the best!

Mary Ann
Oh, I know exactly what my favorite food is: Pasta. All pasta, but especially spaghetti. I like it best in Italy—I went to Italy on vacation last year. The food was wonderful.

Sally
Well, shhh, don't tell anyone … But my very favorite food is chocolate. Chocolate anything—chocolate ice cream, chocolate cookies, chocolate cake with chocolate frosting … but especially a big bar of chocolate. Mmmm. I know it's terrible. Here, have some!

T 9.8 Polite requests

1. Would you like some more carrots?
   Yes, please. They're delicious.
2. Could you pass the salt, please?
   Sure. Here you are.
3. Could I have a glass of water, please?
   Do you want bottled water or tap water?
4. Does anybody want more dessert?
   Yes, please. I'd love some. It's delicious.
5. How would you like your coffee?
   Black, no sugar, please.
6. This is delicious! Can you give me the recipe?
   Yes, of course. I'm glad you like it.
7. Do you want some help with the dishes?
   That's OK. We have a dishwasher.

T 9.9

1. Can I have a cheese sandwich, please?
   Yes, of course. That's $3.50.
2. Could you tell me the time, please?
   It's just after ten.
3. Can you take me to school?
   Sure. Jump in.
4. Can I see the menu, please?
   Here you are. Would you like something to drink?
5. Could you lend me some money, please?
   Not again! How much would you like this time?
6. Can you help me with my homework, please?
   What is it? French? I can't speak a word of French.
7. Can I borrow your dictionary, please?
   Yes, if I can find it. I think it's in my bag.

Unit 10

T 10.1 Listen and repeat.

I'm older than you.
Your class is noisier than my class.
Your car was more expensive than my car.

T 10.2 Much more than …

1. **A** Life in the country is slower than life in the city.
   B Yes, city life is much faster.
2. **A** Los Angeles is safer than London.
   B No, it isn't. Los Angeles is more dangerous.
3. **A** Brasilia is bigger than São Paolo.
   B No, it isn't! It's much smaller.
4. **A** Taipei is more expensive than Tokyo.
   B No, it isn't. Taipei is much cheaper.
5. **A** The buildings in Rome are more modern than the buildings in New York.
   B No, they aren't. They're much older.
6. **A** The subway in New York is better than the Metro in Paris.
   B No! The subway is much worse.

T 10.3 Meg's conversation

T = Tara   M = Meg

T Why did you leave Los Angeles? You had a good job.

M Yes, but I have a much better job here.

T And you had a big apartment in L.A.

M Yeah, but my house here is much bigger.

T Really? How many bedrooms does it have?

M Three. And it has a big yard. It's much cheaper than my apartment in Los Angeles, and it's quieter, too.

T But you don't have any friends in Lakeport!

M I have a lot of new friends. People are much friendlier than in Los Angeles.

T But small towns are so boring.

M Not really. Lakeport is much more interesting than Los Angeles. It has a lot of great stores, a movie theater, and a park. And the air is cleaner, and the streets are quieter and safer than in Los Angeles.

T OK. Everything is better! So when can I visit you?

T 10.4 The biggest and the best

1. That house is very big.
   Yes, it's the biggest house in town.
2. Claridge's is a very expensive hotel.
   Yes, it's the most expensive hotel in London.
3. San Francisco is a beautiful city.
   Yes, it's the most beautiful city in the United States.
4. New York is a very cosmopolitan city.
   Yes, it's the most cosmopolitan city in the world.
5. Tom Hanks is a very popular actor.
   Yes, he's the most popular actor in the United States.
6. Ms. Smith is a very funny teacher.
   Yes, she's the funniest teacher in our school.
7. Ana is a very intelligent student.
   Yes, she's the most intelligent student in our class.
8. This is a very easy exercise.
   Yes, it's the easiest exercise in the book.

T 10.5 Listen and respond.

1. That house is very big.
2. Claridge's is a very expensive hotel.
3. San Francisco is a beautiful city.
4. New York is a very cosmopolitan city.
5. Tom Hanks is a very popular actor.
6. Ms. Smith is a very funny teacher.
7. Ana is a very intelligent student.
8. This is a very easy exercise.

T 10.6 A musical interlude

(*three music excerpts*)

T 10.7 Listen and repeat.

a. woods
b. factory
c. farm
d. field
e. tractor
f. bridge

T 10.8 To the lake

Drive along Park Road and turn right. Go under the bridge and past the church. Turn left up the hill, then turn right after the farm. Drive down the hill to the river. Then go over the bridge. The lake is on the right. It takes 20 minutes.

T 10.9 Norm's drive in the country

Well, I drove out of the garage, along the road, and under the bridge. Then I drove past the church, up the hill, and down the hill. Then I drove over the river, and then—it was terrible—I went through the bushes, and into the lake!

Unit 11

T 11.1 Who's at the party?

A = Alan   M = Monica

A Monica, I don't know any of these people. Who are they?
M Don't worry, Alan. They're all really nice. See that man over there? The one sitting on a stool? That's Harry. He's a musician. He works in L.A.
A Where?
M You know—L.A. Los Angeles.
A Oh, yeah.
M He's talking to Wendy. She's wearing a red dress. She's very nice and very rich! She lives in a beautiful old house in the country.
A Rich, huh?
M Yes. Rich and married! Next to her is Laura. She's drinking a glass of red wine. Laura's my oldest friend. We went to school together.
A And what does Laura do?
M She's a writer. She writes children's stories—they're very good. She's talking to George. He's laughing and smoking a cigar. He's a pilot. He travels the world, thousands of miles every week.
A And who are those two over there? They're dancing. Mmmm. They know each other very well.
M Oh, that's Rita and Sam. They're married. They live in the apartment upstairs.
A So, ummm … that's Harry and that's Wendy and uh … Oh, forget it! I can't remember all those names.

T 11.2 Listen to the questions.

1. Whose baseball cap is this?
2. Whose flowers are these?
3. Whose dog is this?

T 11.3 who's or whose?

1. Who's on the phone?
2. I'm going to the beach. Who's coming?
3. Wow! Look at that sports car. Whose is it?
4. Whose dictionary is this? It's not mine.
5. There are books all over the floor. Whose are they?
6. Who's the most intelligent in our class?
7. Whose book is this?
8. Do you know whose jacket this is?

T 11.4 What a mess!

A Whose tennis racket is this?
B It's mine.
A What's it doing here?
B I'm playing tennis this afternoon.

T 11.5 "What a Wonderful World"

I see skies of green
red roses, too
I see them bloom for me and you
and I think to myself
what a wonderful world.
I see skies of blue
and clouds of white
the bright sunny day
the dark starry night
and I think to myself
what a wonderful world.
The colors of the rainbow
so pretty in the sky
are also on the faces
of the people going by.
I see friends shaking hands
saying, "How do you do?"
They're really saying
"I love you."
I hear babies cry
I watch them grow.
They'll learn much more
than you'll ever know
and I think to myself
what a wonderful world.
Yes, I think to myself
what a wonderful world.

T 11.6 Vowels and diphthongs

Vowels
1. red   said
2. laugh   half
3. list   kissed
4. mean   green
5. foot   put
6. shoes   whose
7. funny   money

Diphthongs
1. white   night
2. brown   town
3. pay   they
4. rose   knows
5. noise   boys

T 11.7 see p. 84

T 11.8 In a clothing store

SP = salesperson   C = customer

SP Can I help you?
C   Yes, I'm looking for a shirt to go with my new suit.
SP What color are you looking for?
C   Blue.
SP How about this one? Do you like it?
C   No, it's not the right blue.
SP Well, what about this one? It's a darker blue.
C   Yes, I like that one much better. Can I try it on?
SP Yes, of course. The fitting rooms are over there. Is the size OK?
C   No, it's too big. Do you have a smaller size?
SP I'm sorry. That's the last blue one we have. But we have a smaller size in white.
C   OK. I'll take the white. How much is it?
SP $34.99. How do you want to pay?
C   Can I pay by credit card?
SP Credit card's fine. Thank you very much.

Unit 12

T 12.1

Nadia
When I grow up, I'm going to be a ballet dancer. I love dancing. I go dancing 3 times a week. I'm going to travel all over the world, and I'm going to learn French and Russian because I want to dance in Paris and Moscow. I'm not going to marry until I'm 35 and then I'm going to have 2 children. I'd like a girl first, and then a boy—but maybe I can't plan that! I'm going to work until I'm 75. I'm going to teach dancing, and I'm going to open a dance school. It's all very exciting.

Ms. Bishop
When I retire … umm well, … 2 things. First, I'm going to learn Russian—I can already speak French and Spanish, and I want to learn another language. And second, I'm going to learn to drive. It's terrible that I'm 59 and I can't drive—no time to learn. Then I'm going to buy a car, and travel all over the world. Also I'm not going to wear boring clothes any more. I hate the skirts and blouses I wear every day for school. I'm going to wear jeans and T-shirts all the time. And when I return from my travels, I'm going to write a book and go on TV to talk about it. I'm going to become a TV star!

T 12.2 see p. 87

T 12.3 Questions about Nadia

1. A Why is she going to learn French and Russian?
   B Because she wants to dance in Paris and Moscow.
2. A When is she going to marry?
   B Not until she's 35.
3. A How many children is she going to have?
   B Two.
4. A How long is she going to work?
   B Until she's 75.
5. A What is she going to teach?
   B Dancing.

T 12.4 Listen and check.

1. Take an umbrella. It's going to rain.
2. Look! Jack's on the wall. He's going to fall.
3. Anna's running very fast. She's going to win the race.
4. Look at the time! You're going to be late for the meeting.
5. Look at that man! He's going to jump.
6. They're going to have a baby. It's due next month.
7. There's my sister and her boyfriend! Yuck! They're going to kiss.
8. Oh, dear. I'm going to sneeze. *Aaaa-chooo!* Bless you!

T 12.5 Listen and check.

MB First I'm going to London.
H Why?
MB To ride on a double-decker bus, of course!
H Oh, yes! How wonderful! Where are you going after that?
MB Well, then I'm going to Paris to see the Eiffel Tower.

T 12.6 The weather

A What's the weather like today?
B It's snowing and it's very cold.
A What was it like yesterday?
B Oh, it was cold and cloudy.
A What's it going to be like tomorrow?
B I think it's going to be warmer.

T 12.7 Conversations about the weather

1. A It's a beautiful day! What should we do?
   B Let's play tennis!
2. A It's raining again! What should we do?
   B Let's stay home and watch a video.

T 12.8

1. A It's a beautiful day! What should we do?
   B Let's play tennis!
   A Oh, no! It's too hot to play tennis.
   B Well, let's go to the beach.
   A OK. I'll get my bathing suit.
2. A It's raining again! What should we do?
   B Let's stay home and watch a video.
   A But we just watched a video last night.
   B Well, let's go to the movies.
   A OK. What movie do you want to see?

Unit 13

T 13.1 General knowledge quiz

1. When did the first person walk on the moon?
   In 1969.
2. Where are the Alps?
   In Europe.
3. Who lives at 1600 Pennsylvania Avenue in Washington, D.C.?
   The president of the United States.
4. Who won the 1994 World Cup?
   Brazil.
5. How many states are there in the United States?
   Fifty.
6. How much does an African elephant weigh?
   5–7 tons.
7. How far is it from Tokyo, Japan, to New York City?
   15,000 kilometers.
8. How old was Princess Diana when she died?
   Thirty-six.
9. What languages do Canadians speak?
   English and French.
10. What did Marconi invent in 1901?
    The radio.
11. What kind of music did Louis Armstrong play?
    Jazz.
12. What happens at the end of *Romeo and Juliet*?
    Romeo and Juliet kill themselves.
13. What happened to Nelson Mandela in 1994?
    He became president of South Africa.
14. Why do birds migrate?
    Because the winter is cold.
15. Which was the first country to have TV?
    Britain.
16. Which language has the most words?
    English.

T 13.2 Listen carefully

1. Why do you want to go?
2. Who is she?
3. Where's she staying?
4. Why didn't they come?
5. How old was she?
6. Does he play the guitar?
7. Where did you go to school?

T 13.3 Noises in the night

It was about 2 o'clock in the morning, and suddenly I woke up. I heard a noise. I got out of bed and went slowly downstairs. There was a light on in the living room. I listened carefully. I could hear two men speaking very quietly. "Burglars!" I thought. "Two burglars!" Immediately I ran back upstairs and called the police. I was really frightened. Fortunately the police arrived quickly. They opened the front door and went into the living room. Then

they came upstairs to find me. "It's all right now, sir," they explained. "We turned the television off for you!"

T 13.4 see p. 98

T 13.5 see p. 100

T 13.6 Catching a train

Trains from Boston South Station to New York Pennsylvania Station. Monday to Friday. Here are the departure times from Boston and arrival times in New York City:
7:55 arriving one o'clock
10:30 arriving 3:35
12:30 arriving 6:20
2:17 …

T 13.7 The information desk

A Good morning. Can you tell me the times of trains from New York back to South Station, please?
B When do you want to come back? Afternoon? Evening?
A About five o'clock this afternoon.
B About five o'clock. Let's see … Well, there's a train that leaves New York at 4:30 … then there isn't another one until 6:45.
A And what time do they get in?
B The 4:30 train gets in to South Station at 9:15 and the 6:40 gets in at 11:25.
A OK. Thanks a lot.

T 13.8

A Hello. A round-trip ticket to New York, please.
C How do you want to pay?
A Cash, please.
C That's 85 dollars.
A Here's a hundred.
C Here's your change and your ticket.
A Thank you. Which platform is it?
C Platform 1. Over there.
A Thank you.

Unit 14

T 14.1 see p. 102

T 14.2 see p. 102

T 14.3 The life of Ryan

Yes, I've lived in a foreign country—in Japan. I lived in Osaka for a year. I enjoyed it very much. I loved the food. And, yes, I've worked for a big company. I worked for Nissan, the car company—that's why I was in Japan. That was two years ago. Then I got another job. Have I stayed in an expensive hotel? No, never—only cheap hotels for me, I'm afraid. But I have flown in a jumbo jet four or five times—but not first class. Business class, but not first!

Oh, I've never cooked a meal for a lot of people. I love food, but I don't like cooking. Sometimes I cook for my girlfriend, but she likes it better if we go out to eat! And I've never met a famous person—oh, just a minute, well not met but I've seen one … I saw a famous politician at the airport once—who was it? I can't remember his name.

I've only seen one Shakespeare play, when I was in high school, we saw *Romeo and Juliet*. It was OK.

I've driven a tractor—I had a summer job on a farm when I was 17. I enjoyed that. Good news—I've never been to the hospital. I was born in a hospital, of course, but that's different. Bad news—I've never won a contest. In fact, I've never won anything! I play the lottery every week but I've never, ever won a thing!

T 14.4 A honeymoon in New York

M = Marilyn J = Judy

M We're having a great time!

J Tell me about it! What have you done so far?

M Well, we went to the top of the Empire State Building. That was the first thing we did. It's right in the center of New York! You can see the whole city from there.

J Have you seen the Statue of Liberty yet?

M Yeah, we have. We took a boat there. It was wonderful. Crowded, but wonderful. That was yesterday. This morning we're going to take a walk around Central Park, then this afternoon we're going shopping on Fifth Avenue. Tomorrow we're going to visit Greenwich Village and Chinatown.

J Wow! You're busy! And what about Rockefeller Center? Have you been there yet?

M No, not yet. It's on Fifth Avenue. We're going to go there tomorrow afternoon and go ice-skating.

J Tomorrow's your last night. What are you going to do on your last night?

M Well, we're going to see a Broadway show, but we haven't decided what to see yet.

J You're so lucky! Give my love to Rod!

M I will. Bye, Judy. See you soon!

T 14.5 "Leaving on a Jet Plane"

My bags are packed, I'm ready to go,
I'm standing here outside your door,
I hate to wake you up and say good-bye,
But the dawn is breaking,
It's early morn',
The taxi's waiting,
He's blowing his horn,
Already I'm so lonesome
I could die.

Chorus
So kiss me and smile for me,
Tell me that you'll wait for me,
Hold me like you'll never let me go,
'Cause I'm leaving on a jet plane,
I don't know when I'll be back again.
Oh, babe, I hate to go.

There's so many times I've let you down,
So many times I've played around,
I tell you now
They don't mean a thing.
Every place I go I'll think of you
Every song I sing, I'll sing for you
When I come back
I'll wear your wedding ring.

T 14.6 Flight information

May I have your attention please? United Airlines flight 823 to Seattle is now boarding at Gate 14. Final boarding announcement for United Airlines Flight 823 to Seattle.

American Airlines flight 516 to Los Angeles is delayed for one hour due to weather. We apologize for any inconvenience.

Northwest flight 726 to Detroit is now boarding at gate 4. Northwest flight 726 to Detroit, now boarding, gate 4.

Air Canada flight 98 to Winnepeg is on time and will board at gate 20.

Delta flight 609 to Atlanta will have a gate change. Please wait in the departure lounge for a further announcement.

Passengers are reminded to keep their hand luggage with them at all times. Thank you.

T 14.7 Conversations at the airport

1. **A** Listen! United flight 823 to Seattle. That's our flight.
   B Did the announcement say Gate 4 or 14?
   A I couldn't hear. I think it said 14.
   B Look! There it is on the monitor. It *is* gate 14.
   A OK. Come on! Let's go.

2. **A** Can I have your ticket, please?
   B Yes, of course.
   A Thank you. How many suitcases do you have?
   B Just one.
   A Any carry-on luggage?
   B Just this bag.
   A That's fine.
   B Oh … Can I have a window seat?
   A Sure … OK. Seat 12A. Here's your boarding pass. Have a nice flight!

3. **A** Rod! Marilyn! Over here!
   B Hi, Judy! Great to see you!
   A It's great to see you, too. You look terrific! Did you have a good time in New York?
   B Fantastic. Everything was great.
   A Well, you haven't missed anything here. Nothing much has happened at all!

4. **A** Well, that's my flight. It's time to go.
   B It's been a wonderful two weeks. I can't believe it's over.
   A I know. When can we see each other again?
   B Soon, I hope. I'll write every day.
   A I'll call, too. Good-bye.
   B Good-bye. Give my love to your family.

Grammar Reference

Unit 1

1.1 Verb *to be*

Affirmative

I	am		
He She It	is		from the U.S.
We You They	are	We're = We are	

I'm = I am

He's = He is
She's = She is
It's = It is

You're = You are
They're = They are

Question

	am	I	
Where	is	he she it	from?
	are	we you they	

I'm 20

I'm 20.
I'm 20 years old.   NOT   ~~I'm 20 years.~~
                            ~~I have 20 years.~~

1.2 Possessive adjectives

What's	my your his	name?
This is	her its our your their	house.

What's = What is

1.3 Question words

What is your phone number?
Where are you from?
How are you?

1.4 *a/an*

It's a	ticket. newspaper. magazine.

We use *an* before a vowel sound.

It's an	apple. envelope. English dictionary.

an hour

I'm a doctor.   NOT   ~~I'm doctor.~~
I'm a student.   ~~I'm student.~~

1.5 Plural nouns

1. Most nouns add *-s* in the plural.
   stamp**s**
   key**s**
   camera**s**

2. If the noun ends in *-s, -ss, -sh,* or *-ch*, add *-es*.
   bus   bus**es**
   class   class**es**
   wish   wish**es**
   match   match**es**

3. If the noun ends in a consonant + *-y*, the y changes to *-ies*.
   country   countr**ies**
   party   part**ies**
   But if the noun ends in a vowel + *-y*, the *-y* doesn't change.
   key   key**s**
   day   day**s**

4. Some nouns are irregular. Dictionaries show this.
   child   children
   person   people
   woman   women
   man   men

1.6 Numbers 1–20

1 one
2 two
3 three
4 four
5 five
6 six
7 seven
8 eight
9 nine
10 ten
11 eleven
12 twelve
13 thirteen
14 fourteen
15 fifteen
16 sixteen
17 seventeen
18 eighteen
19 nineteen
20 twenty

1.7 Prepositions

Where are you **from**?
I live **in** a house **in** Toluca.
What's this **in** English?

Unit 2

2.1 Verb *to be*

Questions with question words

What	is her last name? is his job? is her address?	
Where	is she are you are they	from?
Who	is Laura? is she?	
How old	is he? are you?	
How much	is a brownie?	

Answers

Anderson.
He's a police officer.
82 Hill Road.

Mexico.

She's Patrick's daughter.

Twenty-two.

One seventy-five.

Yes/No questions

Is	he she it	hot?
Are	you they	married?

Short answers

Yes, he is.
No, she isn't.
Yes, it is.

No, I'm not./No, we aren't.
Yes, they are./No, they aren't.

Negative

I	'm not	
He She It	isn't	from the U.S.
We You They	aren't	

I'm not = I am not (I amn't)

He isn't = He is not
She isn't = She is not
It isn't = It is not

We aren't = We are not
You aren't = You are not
They aren't = They are not

2.2 Possessive *'s*

My wife**'s** name is Judy.
That's Andrea**'s** dictionary.

2.3 Numbers 21–100

21 twenty-one
22 twenty-two
23 twenty-three
24 twenty-four
25 twenty-five
26 twenty-six
27 twenty-seven
28 twenty-eight
29 twenty-nine
30 thirty
31 thirty-one
40 forty
50 fifty
60 sixty
70 seventy
80 eighty
90 ninety
100 one hundred

2.4 Prepositions

This is a photo **of** my family.
It's good practice **for** you.

I'm **at** home. My mother and father are **at** work.
I'm **at** La Guardia Community College.

I'm **in** New York. I'm **in** a class **with** eight other students.
I live **in** an apartment **with** two American girls.
Central Park is beautiful **in** the snow.

Unit 3

3.1 Present Simple *he, she, it*

1. The Present Simple expresses a fact which is always true, or true for a long time.

   He **comes** from Taiwan.
   She **works** in a bank.

2. It also expresses a habit.

   He **likes** playing tennis.
   She **has** no free time.

Affirmative

He She It	lives	in Kenya.

Have is irregular.   She **has** a dog.   NOT   she ~~haves~~

Negative

He She It	doesn't live	in Japan.

doesn't = does not

Question

Where does	he she it	live?

Yes/No questions

Does	he she it	live	in Kenya? in Japan?

Short answers

Yes, he does.
No, she doesn't.
Yes, it does.

3.2 Spelling of the third person singular

1. Most verbs add *-s* in the third person singular.

wear	wear**s**
speak	speak**s**
live	live**s**

   But *go* and *do* are different. They add *-es*.

go	go**es**
do	do**es**

2. If the verb ends in *-s*, *-sh*, or *-ch*, add *-es*.

finish	finish**es**
watch	watch**es**

3. If the verb ends in a consonant + *-y*, the *y* changes to *-ies*.

fly	fl**ies**
study	stud**ies**

   But if the verb ends in a vowel + *-y* the *y* does not change.

play	play**s**

4. *Have* is irregular.

have	has

3.3 Prepositions

She lives **in** Kenya.
He rides his bicycle **in** his free time.
In the evening we have supper.
A nurse looks **after** people **in** hospital.
She likes going **for** walks **in** summer.

Get **on** the bus.
He lives **on** an island **in** the west of Scotland.

He gets the mail **from** the boat.
He delivers the beer **to** the pub.
He drives the children **to** school.
At ten we go **to** bed.
He likes listening **to** music.
She speaks **to** people **on** her radio.
She's married **to** an American.

There's a letter **for** you.
He makes breakfast **for** the guests.
He writes **for** a newspaper.

He works **as** an undertaker.
Tourists come **by** boat.
It's **about** 6:30.

Unit 4

4.1 Present Simple

Affirmative

I You We They	start	
He She It	starts	at 6:30.

Negative

I You We They	don't		
He She It	doesn't	start	at 6:30.

Question

When	do	I you we they	start?
	does	he she it	

Yes/No questions

Do	you they	have	a camera?
Does	he she it	like	Chinese food?

Short answers

No, I don't./No, we don't.
Yes, they do.

Yes, he does.
No, she doesn't.
Yes, it does.

4.2 Adverbs of frequency

0%		50%		100%
never	sometimes	often	usually	always

1. These adverbs usually come before the main verb.
   I **usually** go to bed at about 11:00.
   I don't **often** go swimming.
   She **never** eats meat.
   We **always** have wine in the evenings.
   I **sometimes** play tennis on Saturdays.

2. *Sometimes* and *usually* can also come at the beginning or the end of a sentence.
   Sometimes we play cards.   We play cards **sometimes**.
   Usually I walk to school.   I walk to school **usually**.

3. *Never* and *always* can't come at the beginning or the end of a sentence.
   NOT   ~~Never I go to the theater.~~
          ~~Always I have coffee in the morning.~~

4.3 *like/love* + verb + *-ing*

When *like* and *love* are followed by a verb, it is usually verb + *-ing*.
   I **like** cook**ing**.
   She **loves** listen**ing** to music.
   They **like** sail**ing** very much.

4.4 Prepositions

She gets up early **on** weekdays.
He plays soccer **on** Friday mornings.
They never go out **on** Friday evenings.
Where do you go **on** vacation?
He lives **on** the next block.
He hates watching soccer **on** television.

Do you relax **on** weekends?
She gets up **at** six o'clock.

She gets up early **in** the morning.
We go out **in** the evening.
He takes photographs **in** (the) spring.

Unit 5

5.1 *There is/are*

Affirmative

There	is	a sofa.	(singular)
	are	two books.	(plural)

Negative

There	isn't	an armchair.	(singular)
	aren't	any flowers.	(plural)

Yes/No questions

Is	there	a table?
Are		any pictures?

Short answers

Yes, there is.
No, there isn't.

Yes, there are.
No, there aren't.

5.2 *How many . . . ?*

How many books do you have?

5.3 *some/any*

Affirmative
There are **some** flowers.   *some* + plural noun

Negative
There aren't **any** cups.   *any* + plural noun

Question
Are there **any** books?   *any* + plural noun

5.4 this, that, these, those

We use *this* and *these* to talk about people/things that are near to us.
> I like **this** ice cream.
> I want **these** shoes.

We use *that* and *those* to talk about people/things that aren't near to us.
> Do you like **that** picture on the wall?
> Who are **those** children outside?

5.5 Prepositions

It's the best home **in** the world.
The front door is **at** the top of the steps.
There are magazines **under** the table.

There is a photo **on** the television.
There are two pictures **on** the wall.
The movie theater is **on** the left, **across from** the newsstand.

The bank is **next to** the supermarket.
The bus stop is **near** the park.
There is a mail box **in front of** the post office.

Unit 6

6.1 can/can't

Can and *can't* have the same form in all persons.
There is no *do* or *does*.
Can is followed by the infinitive (without *to*).

could/couldn't

Could is the past of *can*. *Could* and *couldn't* have the same form in all persons.
Could is followed by the infinitive (without *to*).

Affirmative

I He/She/It We You They	can could	swim.

Negative

I He/She/It We You They	can't couldn't	dance.

NOT   He ~~doesn't can~~ dance.

Question

What	can could	I you he/she/it we they	do?

Yes/No questions

Can Could	you she they	drive? cook?

Short answers

No, I can't./No, we couldn't.
Yes, she can/could.
Yes, they can/could.

NOT   ~~Do you can~~ drive?

6.2 was/were

Was/were is the past of *am/is/are*.

Affirmative

I He/She/It	was	in Chicago yesterday. in Mexico last year.
We You They	were	

Negative

I He/She/It	wasn't	at school yesterday. at the party last night.
We You They	weren't	

Question

Where	was	I? he/she/it?
	were	we? you? they?

Yes/No questions

Was	he she	at work?
Were	you they	at home?

Short answers

No, he wasn't.
Yes, she was.
Yes, I was./Yes, we were.
No, they weren't.

was born

Where	was	she he	born?
	were	you they	

I **was born** in Brooklyn in 1980.   NOT   ~~I am born~~ in 1980.

6.3 Prepositions

They were **in** Canada in 1998.
I was **at** a party.
Yesterday there was a party **at** my house.
Can I speak **to** you?
She sells pictures **for** $10,000.
She paints **for** two hours **until** bedtime.

Unit 7

7.1 Past Simple — spelling of regular verbs

1. The normal rule is to add -ed.
   work**ed**   start**ed**
   If the verb ends in -e, add -d.
   live**d**   love**d**

2. If the verb has only one syllable and one vowel and one consonant, double the consonant.
   sto**pp**ed   pla**nn**ed

3. Verbs that end in a consonant + -y change to -ied.
   stud**ied**   carr**ied**

7.2 Past Simple

The Past Simple expresses a past action that is finished.
   I **lived** in Seoul when I was 6.
   She **started** work when she was 8.
The form of the Past Simple is the same in all persons.

Affirmative

I He/She/It We You They	moved went	to Atlanta in 1985.

Negative

We use *didn't* + infinitive (without *to*) in all persons.

I He/She/It We You They	didn't	move go	to Atlanta.

Question

We use *did* + infinitive (without *to*) in all persons.

When Where	did	I you he/she/it we they	go?

Yes/No questions

Did	you she they etc.	like enjoy	the movie? the party?

Short answers

No, I didn't./No, we didn't.
Yes, she did.
No, they didn't.

There is list of irregular verbs on p. 142.

7.3 Time expressions

last	night Saturday week month year
yesterday	morning afternoon evening

7.4 Prepositions

She thinks **about** her past life.
She died **in** a car crash.
He was tired **of** politics.
He became interested **in** politics.
He retired **from** politics **in** 1999.
Who is the card **from**?
She worked **from** 6:00 **until** 10:00.

Unit 8

8.1 Past Simple

Negative

Negatives in the Past Simple are the same in all persons.

I He/She We You They	didn't	go out see Tom watch TV	last night.

ago

I went to Brazil	ten years two weeks a month	ago.

8.2 Time expressions

in	the twentieth century 1924 the 1990s winter/summer the evening/the morning September
on	October 10 Christmas Day Saturday Sunday evening weekends
at	seven o'clock night

8.3 Prepositions

What's **on** television this evening?
I'm **on** a cell phone.
We spoke for an hour **on** the phone.
Some people try to find love **on** the Internet.
We didn't laugh **at** his joke.
There was a knock **at** the door.

Unit 9

9.1 Count and noncount nouns

Some nouns are countable.
   a book two books
   an egg six eggs
Some nouns are uncountable.
   bread rice
Some nouns are both!
   Do you like ice cream?
   We'd like three ice creams, please.

9.2 *would like*

Would is the same in all persons. We use *would like* in offers and requests.

Affirmative

I You He/She/It We They	'd like	a drink.	'd = would

Yes/No questions

Would	you he/she/it they	like a cookie?

Short answers

Yes, please.
No, thank you.

9.3 *some* and *any*

We use *some* in affirmative sentences with uncountable nouns and plural nouns.

There is	some	bread	on the table.
There are		oranges	

We use *some* in questions when we ask for things and offer things.

Can I have	some	coffee, please?	(I know there is some coffee.)
Would you like		grapes?	(I know there are some grapes.)

We use *any* in questions and negative sentences with uncountable nouns and plural nouns.

Is there		water?	(I don't know if there is any water.)
Does she have	any	children?	(I don't know if she has any children.)
I can't see		rice.	
There aren't		people.	

9.4 *How much . . . ?* and *How many . . . ?*

We use *How much … ?* with noncount nouns.
   How much rice is there?
   There isn't much rice.
We use *How many … ?* with count nouns.
   How many apples are there?
   There aren't many apples.

9.5 Prepositions

I have a book **by** John Grisham.
Help me **with** my homework.

Unit 10

10.1 Comparative and superlative adjectives

	Adjective	Comparative	Superlative
One-syllable adjectives	old safe big hot	old**er** safe**r** big**ger** hot**ter**	the old**est** the safe**st** the big**gest*** the hot**test***
Adjectives ending in -*y*	noisy dirty	nois**ier** dirt**ier**	the nois**iest** the dirt**iest**
Adjectives with two or more syllables	boring beautiful	**more** boring **more** beautiful	the **most** boring the **most** beautiful
Irregular adjectives	good bad far	**better** **worse** **farther**	the **best** the **worst** the **farthest**

* Adjectives which end in one vowel and one consonant double the consonant.

> You're **older than** me.
> New York is **dirtier than** Paris.
> Montreal is one of **the most beautiful** cities in Canada.

10.2 Prepositions

The country is quieter **than** the city.
The house is 50 meters **from** the sea.
Everest is the highest mountain **in** the world.
He spends his time **on** the banks of the river.
She came **out of** the garage.
He drove **along** the road.
They ran **over** the bridge.
I walked **past** the bank.
He walked **up** the hill.
He ran **down** the hill.
The boat went **across** the river.
The cat ran **through** the bushes.
He jumped **into** the lake.

Unit 11

11.1 Present Continuous

1. The Present Continuous describes an activity happening now.
    > She**'s wearing** jeans.
    > I**'m studying** English.

2. It also describes an activity in the near future.
    > I**'m playing** tennis this afternoon.
    > Jane**'s going** to a party tonight.

Affirmative and Negative

I	am		
He She It	is	(not) going	outside.
We You They	are		

Question

Where	am	I	going?
	is	he/she/it	
	are	we you they	

Yes/No questions

Are you having a good time?
Is my English getting better?
Are they having a party?

Short answers

Yes, we are.
Yes, it is.
No, they aren't.

Spelling of verb + -ing

1. Most verbs just add -ing.
    | wear | wea**ring** |
    | go | go**ing** |
    | cook | cook**ing** |
    | hold | hold**ing** |

2. If the infinitive ends in -e, drop the -e.
    | write | wri**ting** |
    | smile | smil**ing** |
    | take | tak**ing** |

3. When a one-syllable verb has one vowel and ends in a consonant, double the consonant.
    | sit | si**tt**ing |
    | get | ge**tt**ing |
    | run | ru**nn**ing |

11.2 Present Simple and Present Continuous

1. The Present Simple describes things that are always true, or true for a long time.
    > I **come** from Taiwan.
    > He **works** in a bank.

2. The Present Continuous describes activities happening now, and temporary activities.
    > Why **are you wearing** a suit? You usually wear jeans.

11.3 *Whose* + possessive pronouns

Whose ... ? asks about possession.

Subject	Object	Adjective	Pronoun
I	me	my	mine
You	you	your	yours
He	him	his	his
She	her	her	hers
We	us	our	ours
They	them	their	theirs

Whose is this book? Whose book is this? Whose is it?	It's	mine. yours. hers. his. ours. theirs.

11.4 Prepositions

I read **in** bed.
We have this sweater **in** red.
He's talking **to** Mandy.
There's a girl **with** blonde hair.
I'm looking **for** a sweater.
I always pay **by** credit card.

Unit 12

12.1 *going to*

1. *Going to* expresses a person's plans and intentions.
    > She's **going to** be a ballet dancer when she grows up.
    > We're **going to** visit Ayer's rock in Australia this summer.

2. Often there is no difference between *going to* and the Present Continuous to refer to a future intention.
    > I'm **seeing** Peter tonight.
    > I'm **going to see** Peter tonight.

3. We also use *going to* when we can see now that something is sure to happen in the future.
    > Careful! That glass is **going to** fall!

Affirmative and negative

I	am		
He/She/It	is	(not) going to	have a break.
We You They	are		stay at home.

Question

	am	I		
When	is	he/she/it	going to	have a break?
	are	we you they		stay at home?

With the verbs *to go* and *to come*, we usually use the Present Continuous for future plans.
> We're **going** to San Francisco next week.
> Joe and Tim **are coming** for lunch tomorrow.

12.2 Infinitive of purpose

The infinitive can express why a person does something.
> I'm saving my money **to buy** a CD player.
> (= because I want to buy a CD player)

> We're going to Paris **to see** the Eiffel Tower.
> (= because we want to see the Eiffel Tower)

> NOT
> I'm saving my money ~~for to buy~~ a CD player.
> I'm saving my money ~~for buy~~ a CD player.

12.3 Prepositions

I'm going to Florida **in** a year's time.
She's interested **in** flying.
She's good **at** singing.
She was afraid **of** cars.
What's the weather **like**?
What's **on** TV tonight?
There's a movie **on** Channel 4.
What's **on at** the movie theater?

Unit 13

13.1 Question forms

When did the first person walk on the moon?
Where are the Alps?
Who did she marry?
Who was Marconi?
How do you get to school?
What do you have for breakfast?
What happens at the end of the story?
Why do you want to learn English?

How many people are there in the class?
How much does she earn?
How far is it to the center?
What kind of car do you have?
Which newspaper do you read?

13.2 Adjectives and adverbs

Adjectives describe nouns.
> a **big** dog
> a **careful** driver

Adverbs describe verbs.
> She ran **quickly**.
> He drives too **fast**.

To form regular adverbs, add *-ly* to the adjective.
Words ending in *-y* change to *-ily*.

Adjective	Adverb
quick	quickly
bad	badly
careful	carefully
immediate	immediately
easy	easily

Some adverbs are irregular.

Adjective	Adverb
good	well
hard	hard
early	early
fast	fast

13.3 Prepositions

What's the story **about**?
What happens **at** the end of the story?
The train leaves **from** platform 9.

Unit 14

14.1 Present Perfect

1. The Present Perfect refers to an action that happened some time before now.
   She**'s traveled** to most parts of the world.
   Have you ever **been** in a car accident?

2. If we want to say *when* these actions happened, we must use the Past Simple.
   She **went** to Thailand two years ago.
   I **was** in a crash when I was 10.

3. Notice the time expressions used with the Past Simple.

I left	last night.
	yesterday.
	in 1990.
	at three o'clock.
	on Monday.

Affirmative and negative

I You We They	have	(not) been	to Canada.
He She It	has		

I've been = I have been
You've been = You have been
We've been = We have been
They've been = They have been

He's been = He has been
She's been = She has been
It's been = It has been

Question

Where	have	I you we they	been?
	has	she he it	

Yes/No questions
Have you been to Spain?

Short answers
Yes, I have.
No, I haven't.

ever and *never*

We use *ever* in questions and *never* in negative sentences.
   Have you **ever** been to Hong Kong?
   I've **never** been to Hong Kong.

14.2 *yet*

We use *yet* in negative sentences and questions.
   Have you done your homework **yet**?
   I haven't done it **yet** (but I'm going to).

14.3 *been* and *gone*

She's **gone** to Korea (and she's there now).
She's **been** to Korea (sometime in her life, but now she has returned).

14.4 Prepositions

She works **for** a big company.
Hamlet is a play **by** Shakespeare.
Rod and Marilyn are **on** their honeymoon.
Wait **for** me!

Word List

Here is a list of most of the new words in the units of *American Headway 1*.

adj = adjective
adv = adverb
conj = conjunction
opp = opposite
pl = plural
prep = preposition
pron = pronoun
pp = past participle
n = noun
v = verb
infml = informal

Unit 1

alphabet *n* /ˈælfəbɛt/
apartment *n* /əˈpɑrtmənt/
apple *n* /ˈæpl/
Australia *n* /ɔˈstreɪlya/
bag *n* /bæg/
because *conj* /bɪˈkɔz/
Brazil *n* /brəˈzɪl/
brother *n* /ˈbrʌðər/
camera *n* /ˈkæmrə/
Canada *n* /ˈkænədə/
children *n pl* /ˈtʃɪldrən/
dictionary *n* /ˈdɪkʃəˌnɛri/
doctor *n* /ˈdɑktər/
England *n* /ˈɪŋglənd/
English *n* /ˈɪŋglɪʃ/
fine *adj* /faɪn/
France *n* /fræns/
from *prep* /frʌm/
good-bye /ˌgʊdˈbaɪ/
have *v* /hæv/
hello /hɛˈloʊ/
her *pron* /hər/
his *pron* /hɪz/
house *n* /haʊs/
international *adj* /ˌɪntərˈnæʃənl/
Italy *n* /ˈɪtəli/
Japan *n* /dʒəˈpæn/
job *n* /dʒɑb/
key *n* /ki/
Korea *n* /kəˈriə/
language *n* /ˈlæŋgwɪdʒ/
learn *v* /lərn/
letter *n* /lɛtər/
live *v* /lɪv/
magazine *n* /ˈmægəzin/
married *adj* /ˈmærid/
me *pron* /mi/
Mexico *n* /ˈmɛksɪkoʊ/
my *pron* /maɪ/
name *n* /neɪm/
newspaper *n* /ˈnuzpeɪpər/
not bad *adj infml* /ˌnɑt ˈbæd/
orange *n* /ˈɔrɪndʒ/
pretty good *adj infml* /ˌprɪti ˈgʊd/
postcard *n* /ˈpoʊstkɑrd/
Russia *n* /ˈrʌʃə/
see you *v infml* /si yu/
sister *n* /ˈsɪstər/
stamp *n* /stæmp/
student *n* /ˈstudənt/
Taiwan *n* /taɪˈwɑn/
teacher *n* /ˈtitʃər/
telephone number *n* /ˈtɛləfoʊn ˌnʌmbər/
thank you /ˈθæŋk yu/
thanks /ˈθæŋks/
this (book) /ðɪs/
ticket *n* /ˈtɪkɪt/
the United States *n* /ðə yuˈnaɪtəd ˈsteɪts/
the U.S. *n* /ðə yu ɛs/
want *v* /wɑnt/
where *adv* /wɛr/
your *pron* /yər/

Unit 2

accountant *n* /əˈkaʊntnt/
address *n* /ˈædrɛs/
age *n* /eɪdʒ/
American *adj* /əˈmɛrɪkən/
anything else /ˈɛniθɪŋ ˈɛls/
Argentina *n* /ˌɑrdʒənˈtinə/
at home *adv* /æt ˈhoʊm/
aunt *n* /ænt/
awful *adj* /ˈɔfl/
bacon *n* /ˈbeɪkən/
beautiful *adj* /ˈbyutəfl/
big *adj* /bɪg/
bottled water *n* /ˈbɑtld wɔtər/
boyfriend *n* /ˈbɔɪfrɛnd/
brownie *n* /ˈbraʊni/
California *n* /ˌkæləˈfɔrnyə/
Can I have…? /kən aɪ hæv/
Can I help you? /kən aɪ hɛlp yu/
cents *n pl* /sɛnts/
cheap *adj* /tʃip/
chicken *n* /ˈtʃɪkən/
chocolate chip cookie *n* /ˈtʃɑklət tʃɪp ˈkʊki/
class *n* /klæs/
coffee *n* /ˈkɔfi/
coffee bar *n* /ˈkɔfi bɑr/
cold *adj* /koʊld/
college *n* /ˈkɑlɪdʒ/
dancer *n* /dænsər/
daughter *n* /ˈdɔtər/
deli *n* /ˈdɛli/
different *adj* /ˈdɪfrənt/
difficult *adj* /ˈdɪfɪkəlt/
dollar *n* /ˈdɑlər/
drink *n* /drɪŋk/
easy *adj* /ˈizi/
exciting *adj* /ɪkˈsaɪtɪŋ/
expensive *adj* /ɪkˈspɛnsɪv/
fast *adj* /fæst/
father *n* /fɑðər/
first name *n* /ˌfərst ˈneɪm/
french fries *n pl* /ˈfrɛntʃ fraɪz/
friendly *adj* /ˈfrɛndli/
girl *n* /gərl/
girlfriend *n* /ˈgərlfrɛnd/
good *adj* /gʊd/

grandfather *n* /ˈgrænˌfɑðər/
grandmother *n* /ˈgrænˌmʌðər/
hamburger *n* /ˈhæmbərgər/
happy *adj* /ˈhæpi/
here *adv* /hɪr/
here you go /hɪr yə goʊ/
hi /haɪ/
hot *adj* /hɑt/
how much? *adv* /haʊ mʌtʃ/
how old? *adv* /haʊ oʊld/
husband *n* /ˈhʌzbənd/
identity card *n* /aɪˈdɛntəti kɑrd/
Ireland *n* /ˈaɪərlənd/
journalist *n* /ˈdʒərnlɪst/
last name *n* /ˌlæst ˈneɪm/
lettuce *n* /ˈlɛtəs/
love *v* /lʌv/
menu *n* /ˈmɛnyu/
morning *n* /ˈmɔrnɪŋ/
mother *n* /ˈmʌðər/
new *adj* /nu/
nice *adj* /naɪs/
now *adv* /naʊ/
nurse *n* /nɔrs/
old *adj* /oʊld/
orange juice *n* /ˈɔrɪndʒ djʊs/
photo *n* /ˈfoʊtoʊ/
please /pliz/
Poland *n* /ˈpoʊlənd/
police officer *n* /pəˈlis ˈɔfəsər/
practice *v* /ˈpræktɪs/
price *n* /praɪs/
salad *n* /ˈsæləd/
sandwich *n* /ˈsænwɪtʃ/
slow *adj* /sloʊ/
small *adj* /smɔl/
snow *n* /snoʊ/
son *n* /sʌn/
soon *adv* /sun/
speak *v* /spik/
sure *adj* /ʃʊr/
Switzerland *n* /ˈswɪtsərlənd/
tea *n* /ti/
the subway *n* /ðə ˈsʌbweɪ/
tomato *n* /təmˈeɪtoʊ/
tuna *n* /ˈtunə/
uncle *n* /ˈʌŋkl/
understand *v* /ˌʌndərˈstænd/
use *v* /yuz/
vacation *n* /veɪˈkeɪʃn/
who? *pron* /hu/
wife *n* /waɪf/
write *v* /raɪt/
Yeah /yɛə/
young *adj* /yʌŋ/

Unit 3

a little *adj* /ə 'lɪtl/
Africa *n* /'æfrɪkə/
afternoon *n* /ˌæftər'nun/
also *conj* /'ɔlsoʊ/
ambulance *n* /'æmbyələns/
architect *n* /'arkətɛkt/

bartender *n* /'bartɛndər/
be quiet *v* /bi 'kwaɪət/
bed *n* /bɛd/
beer *n* /bɪr/
bicycle *n* /'baɪsɪkl/
boat *n* /boʊt/
boatman *n* /boʊtmən/
breakfast *n* /'brɛkfəst/
building *n* /'bɪldɪŋ/
busy *adj* /'bɪzi/
but *conj* /bʌt/

Canadian *n* /kə'neɪdiən/
chef *n* /ʃɛf/
city *n* /'sɪti/
clock *n* /klak/
come *v* /kʌm/
computer *n* /kəm'pyutər/
cook *v* /kʊk/

day *n* /deɪ/
deliver *v* /dɪ'lɪvər/
design *v* /dɪ'zaɪn/
do *v* /du/
dog *n* /dɔg/
drive *v* /draɪv/

end *v* /ɛnd/
evening *n* /'ivnɪŋ/
every day *adv* /'ɛvri deɪ/
Excuse me /ɪk'skyuz mi/

fire fighter *n* /'faɪər ˌfaɪtər/
fly *v* /flaɪ/
flying doctor *n* /'flaɪɪŋ 'daktər/
food *n* /fud/
free time *n* /fri taɪm/

gas *n* /gæs/
gas station attendant *n*
   /gæs 'steɪʃn ə'tɛndənt/
get up *v* /gɛt ʌp/
glass *n* /glæs/
go *v* /goʊ/
go to bed *v* /goʊ tə bɛd/
guest *n* /gɛst/

help *v* /hɛlp/
hospital *n* /'haspɪtl/
hotel *n* /hoʊ'tɛl/
hour *n* /'aʊər/
house *n* /haʊs/
How's (Ann)? *adv* /haʊz/
hurry up *v* /ˌhəri 'ʌp/

interpreter *n* /ɪn'tərprətər/
island *n* /'aɪlənd/

journalist *n* /'dʒərnəlist/

Kenya *n* /'kɛnyə/

late *adj* /leɪt/
life *n* /laɪf/
like *v* /laɪk/
listen *v* /'lɪsn/
love *v* /lʌv/

mail *n* /meɪl/
mail carrier *n* /'meɪl 'kæriər/
make *v* /meɪk/
man *n* /mæn/
money *n* /'mʌni/
music *n* /'myuzɪk/

never *adv* /'nɛvər/
nonstop *adj* /ˌnan'stap/

office *n* /'ɔfəs/
OK /ˌoʊ'keɪ/
only *adv* /'oʊnli/
ordinary *adj* /'ɔrdnɛri/

pay the bills *v* /peɪ ðə bɪlz/
people *n pl* /'pipl/
perhaps *adv* /pər'hæps/
pilot *n* /'paɪlɪt/
plane *n* /pleɪn/
play *v* /pleɪ/
pump *v* /pʌmp/

radio *n* /reɪdioʊ/
ride *v* /raɪd/

sales assistant *n* /seɪlz ə'sɪstənt/
school *n* /skul/
schoolbus *n* /'skulbʌs/
scientist *n* /'saɪəntɪst/
Scotland *n* /'skatlænd/
sell *v* /sɛl/
serve *v* /sərv/
shop *n* /ʃap/
sick *adj* /sɪk/
sit down *v* /sɪdaʊn/
ski *v* /ski/
soccer *n* /'sakər/
summer *n* /'sʌmər/
supper *n* /'sʌpər/

taxi driver *n* /'tæksi 'draɪvər/
television *n* /'tɛləvɪʒn/
tennis *n* /tɛnɪs/
that's right /ˌðæts 'raɪt/
thing *n* /θɪŋ/
time *n* /taɪm/
tired *adj* /'taɪərd/
too *adv* /tu/
tourist *n* /'tʊrɪst/
town *n* /taʊn/
translate *v* /'trænzleɪt/

undertaker *n* /'ʌndərteɪkər/

vanilla *adj* /və'nɪlə/

walk *v* /wɔk/
watch *n, v* /watʃ/
week *n* /wik/
weekday *n* /'wikdeɪ/
wine *n* /waɪn/
work *v* /wərk/

Unit 4

a lot *adv* /ə 'lat/
after *adv* /'æftər/
always *adv* /'ɔlweɪz/

bad *adj* /bæd/
baseball *n* /'beɪsbɔl/
beach *n* /bitʃ/
block *n* /blak/
brown *adj* /braʊn/
bus *n* /bʌs/
buy *v* /baɪ/

called *pp* /kɔld/
club *n* /klʌb/
color *n* /'kʌlər/

dancing *n* /'dænsɪŋ/
dinner *n* /dɪnr/

early *adj* /'ərli/
especially *adv* /ɪ'spɛʃəli/
export department *n*
   /'ɛksport dɪ'partmənt/
exposures *n pl* /ɪk'spoʊʒərz/

fall *n* /fɔl/
famous *adj* /'feɪməs/
favorite *adj* /'feɪvrɪt/
film *n* /fɪlm/
flower *n* /'flaʊər/
fortunately *adv* /'fɔrtʃənətli/
friend *n* /frɛnd/

game *n* /geɪm/
gold *adj* /goʊld/
gray *adj* /greɪ/
gym *n* /dʒɪm/

hobby *n* /'habi/
how? *adv* /haʊ/

I'm sorry /ˌaɪm 'sari/
ice hockey *n* /'aɪsaki/
ice-skating *n* /'aɪskeɪtɪŋ/
interesting *adj* /'ɪntrəstɪŋ/
interview *v* /'ɪntərvyu/
It doesn't matter /ɪt dəsnt mæʈər/

jogging *n* /dʒagɪŋ/

kid *n* /kɪd/

lake *n* /leɪk/
leisure activity *n*
   /'liʒər æk'tɪvəti/

mean *adj* /min/
meet *v* /mit/
movie *n* /'muvi/

near *adj* /nɪr/
news program *n*
   /nuz 'proʊgræm/
next *adj* /nɛkst/

of course /əv 'koʊrs/
often *adv* /'ɔfn/

Pardon? /pardən/
photograph *n* /'foʊtəgræf/
pick up *v* /pɪk ʌp/

reading n /'ridɪŋ/
Really? /'rili/
red *adj* /rɛd/
relax *v* /rə'læks/

sailing *n* /'seɪlɪŋ/
say *v* /'seɪ/
season *n* /'sizn/
shy *adj* /ʃaɪ/
singing *n* /'sɪŋɪŋ/
smoke *v* /smoʊk/
sometimes *adv* /'sʌmtaɪmz/
song *n* /sɔŋ/
special *adj* /'spɛʃəl/
spring *n* /sprɪŋ/
start *v* /start/
suddenly *adv* /'sʌdənli/
sunbathing *n* /'sʌnbeɪðɪŋ/
sunny *adj* /'sʌni/
swimming *n* /'swɪmɪŋ/

take *v* /teɪk/
That's OK /ˌðæts oʊ'keɪ/
then *adv* /ðɛn/
traffic *n* /'træfɪk/
tree *n* /tri/

usually *adv* /'yuʒəli/

visit *v* /'vɪzɪt/

warm *adj* /warm/
weekend *n* /'wikɛnd/
wet *adj* /wɛt/
What does ... mean?
   /wat dəz ... min/
What time? *adv* /wat 'taɪm/
what? *adv* /wat/
when? *adv* /wɛn/
who? *adv* /hu/
why? *adv* /waɪ/
winter *n* /'wɪntər/

yellow *adj* /'yɛloʊ/

Unit 5

address book *n* /'ædrɛs bʊk/
air conditioning *n* /ɛr kən'dɪʃnɪŋ/
armchair *n* /'ɑrmtʃɛr/

balcony *n* /'bælkəni/
bank *n* /bæŋk/
bathroom *n* /'bæθrum/
bathtub *n* /'bæθtʌb/
bedroom *n* /'bɛdrum/
best *adj* /bɛst/
bookshelf *n* /'bʊkʃɛlf/
bookstore *n* /'bʊkstoʊr/
both /boʊθ/
briefcase *n* /'brifkeɪs/
bus stop *n* /'bʌs stap/

cabinet *n* /'kæbənɪt/
cat *n* /kæt/
CD *n* /si'di/
cell phone *n* /'sɛl foʊn/
champagne *n* /ʃæm'peɪn/
Cheers! /tʃɪrz/
closet *n* /'klazət/
cockpit *n* /'kakpɪt/
coffee table *n* /'kɔfi ,teɪbl/
cup *n* /kʌp/

dishwasher *n* /'dɪʃwaʃər/
door *n* /dɔr/
downstairs *adv* /daʊn'steɪrz/
drugstore *n* /'drʌgstɔr/

emergency exit *n*
    /ɪ'mərdʒənsi 'ɛgzət/
envelope *n* /'ɛnvəloʊp/

far *adv* /far/
first class *adj* /fərst klæs/
flight attendant *n*
    /'flaɪt ə,tɛndənt/
floor *n* /flɔr/
fork *n* /fɔrk/
front door *n* /frʌnt dɔr/

glass *n* /glæs/
grandchildren *n pl*
    /'grændtʃɪldrən/
Grandma *n* /'græma/
grocery store *n* /'groʊsəri stɔr/

home *n* /hoʊm/

in front of *adv* /ɪn frʌnt əv/

kitchen *n* /kɪtʃən/
knife *n* /naɪf/

lady *n* /'leɪdi/
lamp *n* /læmp/
left *adv* /lɛft/
living room *n* /'lɪvɪŋ rum/
luxury *adj* /'lʌkʃəri/

mailbox *n* /'meɪlbax/
mirror *n* /'mɪrər/
modern *adj* /'madərn/
movie theater *n* /'muvi ,θiətər/
music store *n* /'myuzɪk ,stoʊr/

newsstand *n* /'nuzstænd/
next to *adv* /'nɛkstə/
notebook *n* /'noʊtbʊk/

open *v* /'oʊpən/
oven *n* /'ʌvən/

park *n* /park/
party *n* /'parti/
passport *n* /'pæsport/
pay phone *n* /'peɪfoʊn/
pen *n* /pɛn/
picture *n* /'pɪktʃər/
plant *n* /plænt/
plate *n* /pleɪt/
Portugal *n* /'pɔrtʃəgl/
post office *n* /'poʊst ,ɔfɪs/
public rest room *n*
    /'pʌblɪk 'rɛstrum/

refrigerator *n* /rɪ'frɪdʒəreɪtər/
right *adv* /raɪt/
room *n* /rum/
rug *n* /rʌg/

Samoa *n* /sə'moʊə/
shelf *n* /ʃɛlf/
sofa *n* /'soʊfə/
spoon *n* /spun/
steps *n pl* /stɛps/
stereo *n* /'stɛrioʊ/
swimming pool *n* /'swɪmɪŋ pul/

telephone *n* /'tɛləfoʊn/
thanks a lot /'θæŋks ə ,lat/
toilet *n* /'tɔɪlɪt/
top *n* /tɔp/

under *adv* /'ʌndər/
upstairs *adv* /ʌp'steɪrz/

wall *n* /wal/
washing machine *n*
    /'waʃɪŋ mə,ʃin/
window *n* /'wɪndoʊ/
world *n* /'wərld/

yard *n* /yard/

Unit 6

astronaut *n* /'æstrənɔt/
Austria *n* /'ɔstriə/

bedtime *n* /'bɛdtaɪm/
between *adv* /bə'twin/

can't stop *v* /'kænt 'stap/
cartoonist *n* /kar'tunɪst/
check *v* /tʃɛk/
chess *n* /tʃɛs/
Chinese *adj* /tʃaɪ'niz/
concert *n* /'kɔnsərt/
conversation *n* /,kanvər'seɪʃn/

eye *n* /aɪ/
exactly *adv* /ɪg'zækli/

fall in love *v* /fɔl ɪn 'lʌv/
family *n* /'fæmli/
fantastic *adj* /fæn'tæstɪk/
feel *v* /fil/
first *adj* /fərst/
French *adj* /frɛntʃ/
fun *adj* /fʌn/

genius *n* /'dʒinyəs/
Germany *n* /'dʒɛrməni/
give *v* /gɪv/
golf *n* /galf/
great *adj* /greɪt/

hear *v* /hiər/
homework *n* /'hoʊmwərk/

Japanese *adj* /,dʒæpə'niz/
just *adv* /dʒʌst/

know *v* /noʊ/

laugh *v* /læf/
little *adj* /lɪtəl/

manager *n* /'mænədʒər/
message *n* /'mɛsɪdʒ/
month *n* /mʌnθ/

our *pron* /'aʊər/

paint *v* /peɪnt/
painter *n* /'peɪntər/
pianist *n* /'piənɪst/
piano *n* /pi'ænoʊ/
poetry *n* /'poʊətri/
poor *adj* /pɔr/
Portuguese *adj* /,pɔrtʃəgɪz/
practice *v* /præktɪs/

question *n* /'kwɛstʃən/

really *adv* /'rili/

save *v* /seɪv/
sea *n* /si/
see *v* /si/
serious *adj* /sɪriəs/
Spain *n* /speɪn/
Spanish *adj* /'spænɪʃ/
spell *v* /spɛl/
spelling *n* /'spɛlɪŋ/
spend *v* /spɛnd/
still *adv* /stɪl/
style *n* /staɪl/
sun *n* /sʌn/
swim *v* /swɪm/

their *pron* /ðɛr/
think *v* /θɪŋk/
today *adv* /tə'deɪ/
travel *v* /'trævl/
until *conj* /ən'tɪl/

very well *adv* /vɛri wɛl/
video game *n* /'vɪdioʊ geɪm/

was born *v* /wəz bɔrn/
wear *v* /wɛr/
wedding *n* /wɛdɪŋ/
well *adv* /wɛl/

year *n* /yɪr/
yesterday *n* /'yɛstərdeɪ/

Unit 7

army *n* /ˈɑrmi/
bath *n* /bæθ/
become *v* /bəˈkʌm/
birthday *n* /ˈbərθdeɪ/
build *v* /bɪld/

capital *n* /ˈkæpɪtəl/
car crash *n* /ˈkɑr kræʃ/
child *n* /tʃaɪld/
Christmas *n* /ˈkrɪsməs/
college *n* /ˈkɑlɪdʒ/
congratulations *n pl*
    /kənˌgrætʃəˈleɪʃnz/
cotton field *n* /ˈkɑtnfild/
create *v* /kriˈeɪt/

die *v* /daɪ/

earn *v* /ərn/
Easter *n* /ˈistər/
economics *n* /ˌɛkɪˈnɑmɪks/
education *n* /ˌɛdʒəˈkeɪʃn/
end *v* /ɛnd/

farm *n* /fɑrm/
farmer *n* /ˈfɑrmər/
fight *v* /faɪt/
finally *adv* /ˈfaɪnli/
freedom *n* /ˈfridəm/
funeral *n* /ˈfyunərəl/

grandparents *n pl* /ˈgrænpɛrənts/
great grandparents *n pl*
    /ˌgreɪt ˈgrænpɛrənts/
grow *v* /groʊ/

Halloween *n* /ˌhæləˈwin/
hate *v* /heɪt/
head *n* /hɛd/
history *n* /ˈhɪstəri/
horse *n* /hɔrs/

important *adj* /ɪmˈpɔrtnt/
independence *n* /ˌɪndɪˈpɛndəns/

join *v* /dʒɔɪn/

kiss *v* /kɪs/

later *adv* /ˈleɪt̮ər/
law *n* /lɔ/
lawyer *n* /ˈlɔyər/
leader *n* /ˈlidər/
leave *v* /liv/
life *n* /laɪf/
listen *v* /ˈlɪsn/
lose *v* /luz/

midnight *n* /ˈmɪdnaɪt/
million *n* /ˈmɪlyən/
Mother's Day *n* /ˈmʌðərz deɪ/

New Year's Eve *n* /ˌnu yɪrz ˈiv/

own *v* /oʊn/

poem *n* /ˈpoʊəm/
politician *n* /pɑləˈtɪʃn/
politics *n* /ˈpɑlətɪks/
porch *n* /pɔrtʃ/
president *n* /ˈprɛzədənt/
prison *n* /ˈprɪzn/
problem *n* /ˈprɑbləm/

read *v* /rid/
retire *v* /rəˈtaɪər/

same to you /seɪm tə ˈyu/
slave *n* /sleɪv/
soldier *n* /ˈsoʊldʒər/
soon *adv* /sun/
study *v* /ˈstʌdi/
subject *n* /ˈsʌbdʒɛkt/

take a vacation *v*
    /ˌteɪk ə vəˈkeɪʃn/
thank goodness /θæŋk ˈgʊdnəs/
Thanksgiving *n* /θæŋksˈgɪvɪŋ/
the moon *n* /ðəˈmun/
theater *n* /ˈθiət̮ər/
tobacco *n* /təˈbækoʊ/
together *adv* /təˈgeðər/
tomorrow *adv* /təˈmɑroʊ/

university *n* /ˌyunəˈvərsɪti/

Valentine's Day *n*
    /ˈvæləntaɪnz deɪ/
video *n* /ˈvɪdioʊ/
village *n* /ˈvɪlɪdʒ/

war *n* /wɔr/
wedding day *n* /ˈwɛdɪŋ deɪ/
widow *n* /ˈwɪdoʊ/
win *v* /wɪn/

yesterday *adv* /ˈyɛstərdeɪ/

Unit 8

ago *adv* /əˈgoʊ/
arrive *v* /əˈraɪv/
arthritis *n* /ɑrˈθraɪtɪs/
aspirin *n* /ˈæsprɪn/

banana *n* /bəˈnænə/
best-selling *adj* /ˌbɛstsɛlɪŋ/
blue *adj* /blu/
bottle *n* /ˈbɑt̮l/
boy *n* /bɔɪ/

century *n* /ˈsɛntʃəri/
chat *n, v* /tʃæt/
cloth *n* /klɔθ/
clothing *n* /ˈkloʊðɪŋ/
coffee break *n* /ˈkɔfi breɪk/
company *n* /ˈkʌmpəni/

delicious *adj* /dəˈlɪʃəs/
drug *n* /drʌg/

e-mail *n* /ˈimeɪl/
exam *n* /ɪgˈzæm/

fashionable *adj* /ˈfæʃnəbl/
fax *n, v* /fæks/
find *v* /faɪnd/
funny *adj* /ˈfʌni/

get engaged *v* /gɛt ɪngeɪdʒd/
get married *v* /gɛt ˈmærɪd/
green *adj* /grin/

in a hurry *adv* /ɪnəˈhəri/
incredible *adj* /ɪnˈkrɛdɪbl/
Internet *n* /ˈɪntərnɛt/
invent *v* /ɪnˈvɛnt/
invention *n* /ɪnˈvɛnʃn/
inventor *n* /ɪnˈvɛntər/

jeans *n pl* /dʒinz/
joke *n* /dʒoʊk/

listen to *v* /ˈlɪsn tu/

nervous *adj* /ˈnərvəs/

painkiller *n* /ˈpeɪnkɪlər/
philosopher *n* /fəˈlɑsəfər/
produce *v* /prəˈdus/
public holiday *n*
    /ˌpʌblɪk ˈhɑlɪdeɪ/

recipe *n* /ˈrɛsəpi/
record *n* /ˈrekərd/
ride *v* /raɪd/

send *v* /sɛnd/
strong *adj* /strɔŋ/

throw *v* /θroʊ/
transmit *v* /trænsˈmɪt/
true *adj* /tru/

vacuum cleaner *n*
    /ˈvækyum ˌklinər/

way *n* /weɪ/
wear *v* /wɛr/
workman *n* /ˈwərkmən/
workroom *n* /ˈwərkrum/
worried *adj* /ˈwərid/

Unit 9

apple juice *n* /'æpl dʒus/
away from *adv* /ə'weɪ frəm/

banana *n* /bə'nænə/
borrow *v* /'barou/
bread *n* /brɛd/
business *n* /'bɪznɪs/

carrot *n* /'kærət/
cheese *n* /tʃiz/
chicken *n* /'tʃɪkn/
chopsticks *n pl* /'tʃapstɪks/
cigarette *n* /ˌsɪgə'rɛt/
common *adj* /'kamən/
control *v* /kən'troʊl/
course (of a meal) *n* /kɔrs/

delicious *adj* /dɪ'lɪʃəs/
depend on *v* /dɪ'pɛnd an/
dish *n* /dɪʃ/

easily *adv* /'izəli/
egg *n* /ɛg/
environment *n* /ɛn'vaɪərnmənt/

finger *n* /'fɪŋgər/
fish *n* /fɪʃ/
for example /fər ɪg'zæmpl/
foreign *adj* /'fɔrɪn/
fruit *n* /frut/

history *n* /'hɪstəri/
human *adj* /'hyumən/
hungry *adj* /'hʌŋgri/

ice cream *n* /'aɪskrim/

land *n* /lænd/
lend *v* /lɛnd/

main (meal) *adj* /meɪn/
meal *n* /mil/
meat *n* /mit/
middle *n* /'mɪdl/
milk *n* /mɪlk/
mushroom *n* /'mʌʃrum/

noodles *n pl* /'nudəlz/
north *n* /nɔrθ/
nowadays *adv* /'naʊwədeɪz/

part *n* /part/
pasta *n* /'pastə/
pea *n* /pi/
pick up *v* /ˌpɪk 'ʌp/
pizza *n* /'pitsə/
pocket *n* /'pakət/
possible *adj* /'pasəbl/

rice *n* /raɪs/
rich *adj* /rɪtʃ/

salt *n* /sɔlt/
sausage *n* /'sɔsɪdʒ/
sea *n* /si/
seafood *n* /'sifud/
shopping list *n* /'ʃapɪŋ lɪst/
soda *n* /'soʊdə/
south *n* /saʊθ/
spaghetti *n* /spə'gɛʈi/
spicy *adj* /spaɪsi/
strawberry *n* /'strɔberi/
sweet *adj* /swit/

table *n* /'teɪbl/
tap water *n* /'tæp wɔʈər/
tank *n* /tæŋk/
tomato *n* /tə'meɪʈoʊ/
transport *v* /træn'spɔrt/
typical *adj* /'tɪpɪkl/

vegetable *n* /'vɛdʒtəbl/

wonderful *adj* /'wʌndərfl/

yogurt *n* /'yoʊgərt/

Unit 10

actor *n* /'æktər/
air *n* /eɪər/
airport *n* /'eɪərpɔrt/
apartment building *n*
    /ə'partmənt ˌbɪldɪŋ/
art *n* /art/

blues (music) *n pl* /bluz/
boring *adj* /bɔrɪŋ/
bridge *n* /brɪdʒ/
bush *n* /bʌʃ/

carnival *n* /'karnɪvəl/
cheap *adj* /tʃip/
church *n* /tʃərtʃ/
clean *adj* /klin/
cosmopolitan *adj*
    /ˌkazmə'palətn/
cousin *n* /'kʌzn/

dangerous *adj* /'deɪndʒərəs/
dirty *adj* /'dərti/
down *adv* /daʊn/

excellent *adj* /'ɛksələnt/

factory *n* /'fæktəri/
field *n* /fild/
found (a university) *v* /faʊnd/
funny *adj* /fʌni/

garage *n* /gə'raʒ/
gateway *n* /geɪtweɪ/

hill *n* /hɪl/
hymn *n* /hɪm/

immigrant *n* /'ɪməgrənt/
intelligent *adj* /ɪn'tɛlədʒənt/

jazz *n* /dʒæz/

mixture *n* /'mɪkstʃər/
mountain *n* /'maʊntn/
museum *n* /myu'ziəm/
musician *n* /myu'zɪʃn/

nightclub *n* /'naɪtklʌb/
noisy *adj* /'nɔɪzi/

orchestra *n* /'ɔrkəstrə/

parking lot *n* /parkɪŋ lat/
passenger *n* /'pæsɪndʒər/
popular *adj* /'papyələr/
population *n* /ˌpapyə'leɪʃn/
psychiatrist *n* /saɪ'kaɪətrɪst/

quiet *adj* /'kwaɪət/

rich *adj* /rɪtʃ/
river *n* /'rɪvər/
river bank *n* /'rɪvərbæŋk/
road *n* /roʊd/
rock group *n* /'rakgrup/

safe *adj* /seɪf/
seaport *n* /'sipɔrt/
ship *n* /ʃɪp/
short *adj* /ʃɔrt/
skyscraper *n* /'skaɪskreɪpər/
spice *n* /spaɪs/
stand *v* /stænd/
state *n* /steɪt/
sugar *n* /'ʃʊgər/

tall *adj* /tɔl/
the country (= not the city) *n*
    /ðə 'kʌntri/
top ten (music) *n* /ˌtap'ten/
tractor *n* /'træktər/
trade *v* /treɪd/
tunnel *n* /'tʌnl/
turn *v* /tərn/

unfriendly *adj* /ən'frɛndli/

woods *n* /wʊdz/

Unit 11

baby *n* /'beɪbi/
ball *n* /bɔl/
baseball cap *n* /'beɪsbɔl kæp/
blonde *adj* /blɑnd/
bloom *v* /blum/
boots *n pl* /buts/
bright *adj* /braɪt/

chew *v* /tʃu/
choose *v* /tʃuz/
cigar *n* /sɪ'gɑr/
cloud *n* /klaʊd/
coat *n* /koʊt/
credit card *n* /'krɛdɪt kɑrd/
cry *v* /kraɪ/

dark *adj* /dɑrk/
dress *n* /drɛs/

eye *n* /aɪ/

fitting room *n* /'fɪtɪŋ rum/
fresh *adj* /frɛʃ/

good-looking *adj* /ˌgʊd 'lʊkɪŋ/
guest *n* /gɛst/
gum *n* /gʌm/

hair *n* /heɪr/
half *n* /hæf/
hand *n* /hænd/
handsome *adj* /'hænsəm/
hat *n* /hæt/

inline skates *n pl* /ˌɪnlaɪn 'skeɪts/

jacket *n* /dʒækɪt/

long *adj* /lɔŋ/

night *n* /naɪt/

pants *n pl* /pænts/
pretty *adj* /'prɪti̬/

rainbow *n* /'reɪnboʊ/
run *v* /rʌn/

shake *v* /ʃeɪk/
shiny *adj* /'ʃaɪni/
shirt *n* /ʃərt/
shoes *n pl* /ʃuz/
shorts *n pl* /ʃɔrts/
silly *adj* /sɪli/
skateboard *n* /'skeɪtboʊrd/
skirt *n* /skərt/
sky *n* /skaɪ/
smile *v* /smaɪl/
sneakers *n pl* /snikərz/
starry *adj* /'stɑri/
suit *n* /sut/
sunglasses *n pl* /'sʌnglæsɪz/
sweater *n* /'swɛt̬ər/

talk *v* /tɔk/
T-shirt *n* /'tiʃərt/
try *v* /traɪ/

umbrella *n* /ʌm'brɛlə/

white *adj* /waɪt/
whose? *pron* /huz/
wonderful *adj* /'wʌndərfəl/

Unit 12

accident *n* /'æksədənt/
adventure *n* /əd'vɛntʃər/

ballet dancer *n* /bæ'leɪ ˌdænsər/
bathing suit *n* /beɪðɪŋ sut/
Bless you! /'blɛsyu/
blouse *n* /blaʊs/

car racing *n* /'kɑr reɪsɪŋ/
cloudy *adj* /klaʊdi/
computer programmer *n*
    /kəmˌpyutər 'proʊgræmər/
cool *adj* /kul/

danger *n* /'deɪndʒər/
double-decker bus *n*
    /ˌdʌbl dɛkər 'bʌs/
dry *adj* /draɪ/

Egypt *n* /i'dʒɪpt/

foggy *adj* /fɔgi/
forever *adv* /fə'rɛvər/
forget *v* /fər'gɛt/
full-time *adj* /ˌfʌl'taɪm/
future *n* /'fyutʃər/

grades *n pl* /greɪdz/

have a baby *v* /hæv ə 'beɪbi/

India *n* /ɪ'ndiə/

jump *v* /dʒʌmp/

lion *n* /laɪən/

parachute *n* /'pærəʃut/
peaceful *adj* /'pisfəl/
professional *adj* /prə'fɛʃənl/
pyramid *n* /'pɪrəmɪd/

quit *v* /kwɪt/

race *n, v* /reɪs/
race-car driver *n*
    /ˌreɪskɑr 'draɪvər/
racing school *n* /'reɪsɪŋ skul/
rain *n, v* /reɪn/
rainy *adj* /reɪni/
retire *v* /rə'taɪr/

sky diver *n* /'skaɪdaɪvər/
skydiving *n* /'skaɪdaɪvɪŋ/
sneeze *v* /sniz/
snowy *adj* /snoʊwi/

test driver *n* /'tɛst draɪvər/
track *n* /træk/
TV star *n* /ˌtivi 'stɑr/

view *n* /vyu/

wash *v* /waʃ/
weather *n* /wɛðər/
windsurfing *n* /'wɪndsərfɪŋ/
windy *adj* /'wɪndi/

Yuck! /yʌk/

Unit 13

annoyed *adj* /əˈnɔɪd/
annoying *adj* /əˈnɔɪɪŋ/
badly *adv* /ˈbædli/
behave *v* /bəˈheɪv/
behavior *n* /bəˈheɪvyər/
bored *adj* /bɔrd/

carefully *adv* /ˈkɛrfəli/

elephant *n* /ˈɛləfənt/
excited *adj* /ɪkˈsaɪt̮əd/

fluently *adv* /ˈfluəntli/

guitar *n* /gəˈtɑr/

habit *n* /ˈhæbɪt/
hard *adj* /hɑrd/
horribly *adv* /ˈhɔrəbli/

immediately *adv* /ɪˈmidiətli/
interested *adj* /ˈɪntrəstəd/

leather *n* /lɛðər/

mall *n* /mɔl/
marathon *n* /ˈmærəθɑn/
migrate *v* /ˈmaɪgreɪt/

pass the test *v* /ˌpæs ðə ˈtɛst/
pin *v* /pɪn/
platform *n* /ˈplætfɔrm/

quietly *adv* /ˈkwaɪətli/

ridiculous *adj* /rɪˈdɪkyələs/
rose *n* /roʊs/
round-trip *adj* /ˌraʊndˈtrɪp/
rude *adj* /rud/

sheep *n* /ʃip/
slowly *adv* /ˈsloʊli/
station *n* /ˈsteɪʃn/

team *n* /tim/
teenager *n* /ˈtineɪdʒər/
tell a lie *v* /ˌtɛlə ˈlaɪ/
tell a story *v* /ˌtɛlə ˈstoʊri/
the moon *n* /ðə ˈmun/
the Alps *n* /ðə ælps/
timetable *n* /ˈtaɪmteɪbl/
tiring *adj* /taɪərɪŋ/
ton *n* /tʌn/
train *n* /treɪn/

unfortunately *adv* /ʌnˈfɔrtʃənətli/

well-behaved *adj* /ˌwɛlbəˈheɪvd/
whistle *n* /wɪsl/
wolf *n* /wʊlf/
worried *adj* /wɔrid/
worrying *adj* /wɔriɪŋ/

Unit 14

admiral *n* /ˈædmərəl/
airport *n* /ˈɛrpɔrt/
ambulance driver *n*
    /ˈæmbyələns ˌdraɪvər/
announcement *n* /əˈnoʊnsmənt/
arrival area *n* /əˈraɪvl ˌɛriə/

board *v* /bɔrd/
boarding pass *n* /ˈbɔrdɪŋ pæs/

cart *n* /kɑrt/
cashier *n* /ˈkæʃir/
check in *v* /ˈtʃɛkɪn/
contest *n* /ˈkɑntɛst/

dance *n* /dæns/
dawn *n* /dɔn/
departure lounge *n*
    /dəˈpɑrtʃər ˌlaʊnʒ/

exactly *adv* /ɪgˈzæktli/

finally *adv* /ˈfaɪnli/
flag *n* /flæg/
flight *n* /flaɪt/

gate *n* /geɪt/
government *n* /ˈgʌvərmənt/

happen *v* /ˈhæpn/
heart attack *n* /ˈhɑrt ətæk/
honeymoon *n* /ˈhʌnimun/
horn (of a car) *n* /hɔrn/
hospital *n* /ˈhɑspɪtl/

illness *n* /ˈɪlnəs/

jumbo jet *n* /ˌdʒʌmboʊ ˈdʒɛt/
just /dʒʌst/

let you down *v* /lɛt yu ˈdaʊn/
luggage *n* /lʌgɪdʒ/
lung cancer *n* /ˈlʌŋ kænsər/

millionare *n* /ˌmɪlyəˈnɛr/
monitor *n* /ˈmɑnətər/
move *v* /muv/

outside *adv* /ˌaʊtˈsaɪd/

passport control *n*
    /ˈpæspɔrt kənˌtroʊl/

secretary *n* /ˈsɛkrəteɪri/
stroke *n* /stroʊk/
suddenly *adv* /ˈsʌdənli/
suitcase *n* /ˈsutkeɪs/

Thailand *n* /ˈtaɪlænd/
tractor *n* /ˈtræktər/

United Kingdom *n*
    /yuˌnaɪtɪd ˈkɪŋdəm/

wait *v* /weɪt/

yet *adv* /yɛt/

Appendix 1

IRREGULAR VERBS

Base form	Past Simple	Past Participle
be	was/were	been
become	became	become
begin	began	begun
break	broke	broken
bring	brought	brought
build	built	built
buy	bought	bought
can	could	been able
catch	caught	caught
choose	chose	chosen
come	came	come
cost	cost	cost
cut	cut	cut
do	did	done
drink	drank	drunk
drive	drove	driven
eat	ate	eaten
fall	fell	fallen
feel	felt	felt
fight	fought	fought
find	found	found
fly	flew	flown
forget	forgot	forgotten
get	got	gotten
give	gave	given
go	went	gone/been
grow	grew	grown
have	had	had
hear	heard	heard
hit	hit	hit
keep	kept	kept
know	knew	known
leave	left	left
lose	lost	lost
make	made	made
meet	met	met
pay	paid	paid
put	put	put
read /rid/	read /rɛd/	read /rɛd/
ride	rode	ridden
run	ran	run
say	said	said
see	saw	seen
sell	sold	sold
send	sent	sent
shut	shut	shut
sing	sang	sung
sit	sat	sat
sleep	slept	slept
speak	spoke	spoken
spend	spent	spent
stand	stood	stood
steal	stole	stolen
swim	swam	swum
take	took	taken
tell	told	told
think	thought	thought
understand	understood	understood
wake	woke	woken
wear	wore	worn
win	won	won
write	wrote	written

Appendix 2

VERB PATTERNS

Verb + -*ing*	
like	
love	swimming
enjoy	
hate	cooking
finish	
stop	

Verb + *to* + infinitive	
choose	
decide	
forget	
promise	to go
need	
help	
hope	
try	to work
want	
would like	
would love	

Verb + -*ing* or *to* + infinitive	
begin	raining/to rain
start	

Modal auxiliary verbs	
can	
could	go
will	arrive
would	

Phonetic Symbols

Consonants				
1	/p/	as in	**pen**	/pɛn/
2	/b/	as in	**big**	/bɪg/
3	/t/	as in	**tea**	/ti/
4	/d/	as in	**do**	/du/
5	/k/	as in	**cat**	/kæt/
6	/g/	as in	**go**	/goʊ/
7	/f/	as in	**five**	/faɪv/
8	/v/	as in	**very**	/ˈvɛri/
9	/s/	as in	**son**	/sʌn/
10	/z/	as in	**zoo**	/zu/
11	/l/	as in	**live**	/lɪv/
12	/m/	as in	**my**	/maɪ/
13	/n/	as in	**nine**	/naɪn/
14	/h/	as in	**happy**	/hæpi/
15	/r/	as in	**red**	/rɛd/
16	/y/	as in	**yes**	/yɛs/
17	/w/	as in	**want**	/wɑnt/
18	/θ/	as in	**thanks**	/θæŋks/
19	/ð/	as in	**the**	/ðə/
20	/ʃ/	as in	**she**	/ʃi/
21	/ʒ/	as in	**television**	/ˈtelɪvɪʒn/
22	/tʃ/	as in	**child**	/tʃaɪld/
23	/dʒ/	as in	**Japan**	/dʒəˈpæn/
24	/ŋ/	as in	**English**	/ˈɪŋglɪʃ/

Vowels				
25	/i/	as in	**see**	/si/
26	/ɪ/	as in	**his**	/hɪz/
27	/ɛ/	as in	**ten**	/tɛn/
28	/æ/	as in	**stamp**	/stæmp/
29	/ɑ/	as in	**father**	/ˈfɑðər/
30	/ɔ/	as in	**saw**	/sɔ/
31	/ʊ/	as in	**book**	/bʊk/
32	/u/	as in	**you**	/yu/
33	/ʌ/	as in	**sun**	/sʌn/
34	/ə/	as in	**about**	/əˈbaʊt/
35	/eɪ/	as in	**name**	/neɪm/
36	/aɪ/	as in	**my**	/maɪ/
37	/ɔɪ/	as in	**boy**	/bɔɪ/
38	/aʊ/	as in	**how**	/haʊ/
39	/oʊ/	as in	**go**	/goʊ/
40	/ər/	as in	**bird**	/bərd/
41	/ɪr/	as in	**near**	/nɪr/
42	/ɛr/	as in	**hair**	/hɛr/
43	/ɑr/	as in	**car**	/kɑr/
44	/ɔr/	as in	**more**	/mɔr/
45	/ʊr/	as in	**tour**	/tʊr/

Acknowledgments (continued)

The publishers would also like to thank the following for their help:

p. 20 "It's a Job for Nine Men, but Someone's Got To Do It" by Rebecca Fowler. *The Mail Night and Day Magazine*, May 3, 1998. © *The Mail on Sunday*.

p. 37 "The Jet Settler" by Andy Lines. *The Mirror, Cover Magazine*, March 1999. © Mirror Group Newspapers.

p. 45 "Refugee's Daughter Hailed as New Picasso" by Nigel Reynolds. *The Daily Telegraph*, March 12, 1996. © Telegraph Group Ltd.

p. 55 "Happy Birthday to You" by Mildred J.Hill and Patty S. Hill © 1935 (Renewed) Summy-Birchard Music, a Division of Summy-Birchard, Inc. All Rights Reserved. Used By Permission. WARNER BROS. PUBLICATIONS U.S. INC., Miami, FL. 33014

p. 83 "What a Wonderful World." Written by George David Weiss and George Douglas. Published by: Abilene Music, Road Music, and Quartet Music. All Rights Reserved. Used By Permission.

p. 98 "The Story-Teller" from *Tooth and Claw* (Oxford Bookworm Series) by Rosemary Border. Reproduced by permission of Rosemary Border.

p. 107 "Discover the Secrets of a Long Life" by Katy Macdonald, *The Daily Mail*, November 2, 1993. © *The Daily Mail*.

p. 108 "Leaving on a Jet Plane" Words and Music by John Denver. Copyright © 1967; Renewed 1995 Anna Kate Deutschendorf, Zachary Deutschendorf and Jesse Belle Denver for the U.S.A. All Rights for Anna Kate Deutschendorf and Zachary Deutschendorf Administered by Cherry Lane Music Publishing Company, Inc. (ASCAP)
All Rights for Jesse Belle Denver Administered by WB Music Corp. (ASCAP)
All Rights for the world excluding the U.S.A., U.K., Eire, Australia and South Africa Controlled by Cherry Lane Music Publishing Company, Inc. (ASCAP) and DreamWorks Songs (ASCAP)
All Rights for the U.K., Eire, Australia and South Africa Controlled by Essex Music (PRS).
International Copyright Secured. All Rights Reserved.